0

Psychology
First SECOND
EDITION

Psychology
First SECOND EDITION

Barbara Woods

Hodder Arnold

A MEMBER OF THE HODDER HEADLINE GROUP

Orders: please contact Bookpoint Ltd, 130 Milton Park, Abingdon, Oxon OX14 4SB.
Telephone: +44 (0)1235 827720. Fax: +44 (0)1235 400454. Lines are open from
9.00 – 5.00, Monday to Saturday, with a 24-hour message answering service.
You can also order through our website www.hoddereducation.co.uk

If you have any comments to make about this, or any of our other titles, please send
them to educationenquiries@hodder.co.uk

British Library Cataloguing in Publication Data
A catalogue record for this title is available from the British Library

ISBN-10: 0 340 92590 6
ISBN-13: 978 0 340 92590 4

First Edition Published 2001
This Edition Published 2006

Impression number   10 9 8 7 6 5 4 3 2
Year   2009 2008 2007 2006

Hodder Headline's policy is to use papers that are natural, renewable and recyclable
products and made from wood grown in sustainable forests. The logging and
manufacturing processes are expected to conform to the environmental regulations
of the country of origin.

Cover photos from Ilario & Magali/Photonica/Getty Images and Davies &
Starr/The Image Bank/Getty Images.
Typeset by GreenGate Publishing Services, Tonbridge, Kent.
Printed in Spain for Hodder Arnold, an imprint of Hodder Education,
a member of the Hodder Headline Group, 338 Euston Road, London NW1 3BH

Contents

Preface

Psychology First has been written to accompany the OCR specification for GCSE Psychology. This second edition includes more details on evaluation, theories and ethics as well as highlighted evaluation sections and definitions.

My aim has been to write a book which students find clear and interesting, and can use as their main text for the course. Its format reflects the six approaches in the OCR specification, such as social psychology or behavioural psychology. Each approach is represented by two topics and a chapter is devoted to each of them. For example, social psychology is represented by a chapter on Social Influence and another on Environment and Behaviour. In addition to these 12 chapters, there are two more covering research methods and report writing. These will help students to understand how research methods can impact on psychological knowledge and support them as they plan, conduct and write up their course-work. Key terms are given in bold type and explained in the Glossary.

The OCR specification also requires students to show their knowledge of four themes which are important in psychology. These are methodology, ethics, applications and cultural diversity: all four themes appear throughout the book. The main aspects of methodology are explained in chapters 13 and 14 but they also appear in the text wherever there is reference to, for example, an experiment, an observational study, variables or how participants were selected. The second theme is ethics, which refers to the standards of behaviour to which psychologists should adhere in their research. To help identify points concerning ethics there is a smiley face icon alongside the text.

For the third theme, applications, students should have some ideas about how the results of research can be applied and how they can be useful in everyday life. References to applications occur throughout the book, sometimes under evaluation points but also in chapters such as Memory and Attitudes of Prejudice. The final theme, cultural diversity, is included to ensure that reference is made to all kinds of people. Where cultural diversity is discussed it is highlighted by a globe icon alongside the text.

In addition to the ethics and cultural diversity icons, there are three more which flag up particular aspects of the text. The purpose of all icons is described below:

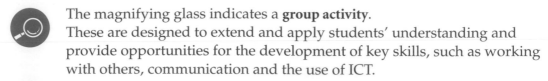
The magnifying glass indicates a **group activity**.
These are designed to extend and apply students' understanding and provide opportunities for the development of key skills, such as working with others, communication and the use of ICT.

The plus/minus icon indicates an **evaluation point**. This gives advantages and disadvantages of a theory, method or application to everyday life.

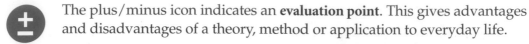
The scales indicate a topic related to **citizenship**.
These should develop students' understanding of issues such as prejudice, conformity, morality and male/female differences.

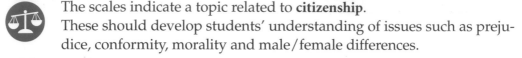
The smiling face indicates **ethical issues**.
These are detailed in the final chapter, but this icon shows where they apply in an everyday or in a research setting.

The globe indicates a topic related to **cultural diversity**.
These are intended to broaden students' awareness of those who rarely appear in general texts, for example those with disabilities, the elderly, people from non-Western cultures.

Each chapter ends with a summary of what the student needs to know for the examination, which has been taken directly from the OCR specification, and several sample exam questions. The reading list provides some suggestions for further reading. The OCR specification provides more detailed information about the examination, coursework, ethical issues, teacher training and further reading. The OCR website is www.ocr.org.uk

Barbara Woods

Acknowledgements

I would like to thank all those who have helped in this second edition, particularly Emma Woolf for her persuasion, Veronica Tighe and Jan England for valuable feedback and ideas, Stephen Parkes at OCR and Jo Lincoln for working magic on the manuscript. Lastly, thanks to Richard for constant support.

Barbara Woods

The author and publishers would like to thank the following for permission to reproduce material in this book: page 5, © William Vandivert; page 10, from the film *Obedience* © 1965 by Stanley Milgram and distributed by Penn State Media Sales; page 22, Romilly Lockyer/The Image Bank/Getty Images; page 23, Dick Makin/Alamy; page 25 (left), Sally and Richard Greenhill; page 25 (right), Arcaid/Alamy; page 36, Norbert Schaefer/Alamy; page 44, © Albert Bandura; page 50, Richard Sellers/Sportsphoto; page 53, © Suhaib Salem/Reuters/Corbis; page 60, © Jerry Tobias/Corbis; page 63, Mike Abrahams; page 65, © Ariel Skelley/Corbis; page 73, Bubbles Photolibrary/Alamy; page 75, NYT Pictures; page 86, The Photolibrary Wales/Alamy; page 91, Gareth Copley/PA/EMPICS; page 93, © Owen Franken/Corbis; page 100, John Fryer/Alamy; page 103, Ric Ergenbright/Corbis; page 107, © Brooks Kraft/Corbis; page 108, © Sally Greenhill/Sally & Richard Greenhill; page 116, © Shannon Stapleton/Reuters/Corbis; page 126, courtesy of Harvard University Archives; page 135, ITV/Rex Features; page 147, picturesbyrob/Alamy; page 153, Oscar Burriel/Science Photo Library; page 161 (left), © Profimedia.CZ s.r.o./Alamy; page 161 (right), Ford Smith/Corbis; page 162, Universal/Everett/Rex Features; page 164, Ulrike Press/Photofusion Picture Library; page 165, © Robbie Jack/Corbis.

The cover image is reproduced courtesy of Ilario & Magali/Photonica/Getty (Chestnut Seed) and Davies & Starr/The Image Bank/Getty (Orange, close-up).

Every effort has been made to obtain necessary permission with reference to copyright material. The publishers apologise if inadvertently any sources remain unacknowledged and will be glad to make the necessary arrangements at the earliest opportunity.

Social Psychology

The primary concern of social psychologists is to understand behaviour in a social context and the ways in which the social context can influence behaviour. This is illustrated in the next two chapters.

Chapter 1 covers Social Influence, which is about how other people can influence our behaviour. Chapter 2 is Environment and Behaviour, which looks at how we regulate our interactions with others.

Social Influence

Psychologists who study social influence want to find out how other people affect our behaviour. Have you ever laughed at a joke which was not funny, simply because everyone else did? You were not asked to laugh, you chose to conform to the norms of the group. At the other extreme, people will sometimes obey others even to the point of killing innocent people. Research suggests that the atrocities in Nazi Germany, Vietnam or the former Yugoslavia could have been performed by many of us. This chapter looks at some of the research which has tried to discover more about why people conform and why they obey.

Conformity

Although most of us like to feel that we make our own decisions, in reality we often conform by adjusting our actions or opinions so that they fit in with those of other people in a group. This is known as **conformity**, which can be defined as:

● changing one's beliefs or behaviour because of real or imagined group pressure.

Sherif's research

One of the earliest studies of conformity was a series of **laboratory experiments** conducted by Muzafer Sherif (1935). He used the autokinetic effect – a visual illusion in which a stationary dot of light appears to move when shown in a very dark room. **Participants** were asked how far they thought the light moved, and those who were alone when they observed the light gave estimates between 2 and 25 cm. Then participants observed the light with two others over a series of trials, and each of them estimated in public how far they thought the light moved. These estimates became closer and closer after each trial: a **group norm** emerged. You can see this in Figure 1.1. Afterwards, each participant observed the light alone and their estimate remained close to the group norm.

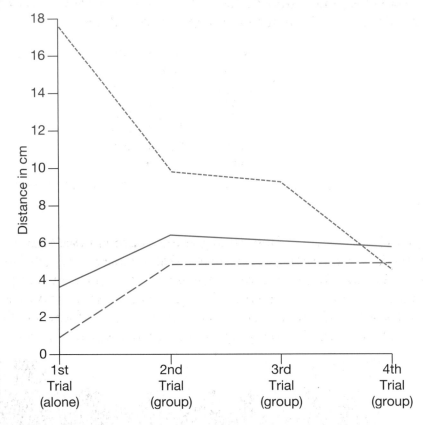

Figure 1.1 Graph showing typical estimates given by Sherif's participants, first individually and then within a group

Evaluation of Sherif's research

A general evaluation of research on Conformity is discussed on p.7. Particular criticism of Sherif's research is that the participants could not be considered a group as there was no interaction between them. Several reported afterwards that they had tried to work out the correct answer and did not feel influenced by the others' estimates. Solomon Asch made the point that they conformed to a group norm simply because they did not know the correct answer.

Asch's research

Asch (1951) was interested in whether an individual would conform to the group even when they knew the group was wrong. He devised a series of **laboratory**

experiments with groups of six to nine people. There was one **participant**, but the rest were **confederates** (they were pretending to be participants) who had been told to give wrong answers on certain trials. Asch said he was testing visual perception and showed the group lines of different lengths (see Figure 1.2). Each person said whether line A, B or C was the same length as the test line.

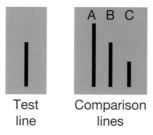

Test line Comparison lines

Figure 1.2 An example of the test line and the comparison lines in an Asch experiment

The participant was one of the last to give his judgement (see Figure 1.3), and in **control trials** when participants were tested alone there were very few wrong answers. But Asch found that when they became part of a group, 25 per cent of participants conformed to the rest of the group on most of the occasions when the group was wrong. Overall, 75 per cent of participants conformed to the wrong answer at least once. The average rate of conformity was 32 per cent.

Figure 1.3 The only person who does not know what is going on is the participant – number 6. In these photographs he is giving his judgement after each of the five men before him have given an obviously wrong answer (from S. Asch, 1958)

When participants were interviewed afterwards most said they knew they were giving the wrong answer but, for example, did not want to look a fool or upset the experiment (this is an example of **demand characteristics**, see p.180). In further trials Asch found that the following factors influenced conformity:

- **Unanimity** – when one other person in the group gave a different answer to the others, and therefore the group answer was not unanimous, conformity dropped. This was true even if that person's answer also seemed to be wrong.
- **Ambiguity** – when the lines were made more similar in length it was harder to judge the correct answer; Asch found that in this case conformity increased.
- **Group size** – levels of conformity were affected by the number of people in the group, as shown in Table 1.1. Because conformity does not increase in groups larger than four, this is considered the optimal group size.

Number of others in group	Average level of conformity by participants
1 confederate	3%
2 confederates	13%
3 confederates	32%
6 confederates (the basic trial)	32%

Table 1.1 Levels of conformity shown by participants in Asch's research

Evaluation of Asch's research

Apart from the general evaluation points detailed on p.7, Asch's method has also been criticised for being slow and expensive. More importantly, it contravenes ethical guidelines by **deceiving** the participants and causing them **distress**, as some were confused and embarrassed.

Another problem is that the results may not generalise, because they could have been a reflection of the high levels of conformity in America during the 1950s. Later replications of Asch's work have generally found lower conformity levels, possibly due to the more liberal climate of the 1960s.

Crutchfield's research

Subsequently, R. Crutchfield (1954) tested conformity in situations where participants answered questions in private. They sat in a booth with a row of lights in front of them; each of the lights was supposed to indicate the answers others had given to the same question. Participants gave answers by pressing a button, which was a much cheaper and faster procedure than Asch's.

Crutchfield found on average about one-third conformity (a similar result to that found by Asch) and also noted that some participants were very conforming and others very independent. As a follow-up, Crutchfield gave his participants personality and IQ tests. He found that those who conformed more were also more likely to be open to the influence of others and be less intellectually competent, perhaps relying more on the judgements of others. These individual differences may go some way to explaining the differences in levels of conformity which both Asch and Crutchfield found.

Evaluation of research on conformity

There are several criticisms of these studies and their conclusions, in particular:

- **Artificiality** – results derive from studies conducted in laboratory settings using stimuli not related to everyday life experiences, for example we rarely have to give a 'correct' answer. Real-life conformity is more about fitting in with others, and the groups to which we belong comprise people we know a little about, unlike the laboratory experiment.

  Not only were the groups artificially created, but in Asch's research the 'participants' did not behave in a normal way. This is evident from an amended version of Asch's experiment which used a group of genuine participants and a **confederate** who gave the wrong answers. When this happened the participants asked if he could see properly, and eventually started laughing. The lack of 'real' behaviour in Asch's confederates emphasised the artificial nature of the experiment.

- **Conformity or independence?** – Sherif, Asch and Crutchfield calculated **mean** levels of conformity which suggested that conformity was fairly high, but more interesting is the large **range** in levels of conformity (for details of means and ranges see p.196). Critics have asked why some people are able to resist group pressure and whether an individual can actually get the rest of the group to change *their* opinions. Questions such as these have been studied under the heading of minority influence.

- **Nature of the task** – most of the early research used male participants, but when Asch's experiment was conducted with females, conformity was even higher. F. Sistrunk and J. McDavid (1971) argued that this was because women were not familiar with the type of task or its setting. Their study showed that men conformed more when asked questions about cooking utensils and women conformed more when asked about tools. In other words, when participants are unsure about the correct answer they look to others, which is what Sherif found.

> **GROUP ACTIVITY** – Conforming to group norms
>
> Each member of the group will ask a few participants a question with no clear answer; for example you could fill a jar with beans and ask how many beans it contains. Each participant will be asked to write their answer on a sheet of paper which lists the answers apparently given by other people.
>
> In fact these answers are ones you have made up. You should provide half your participants with an answer sheet giving low estimates for the number of beans, the other half of your participants with a sheet giving high estimates.
>
> Pool the answers given in the high estimate condition and pool the answers given in the low estimate condition. Calculate the mean and the range of the answers in each condition, then compare them with others in your group. Is there a difference? You could note whether participants are male or female and compare their responses also.

Cultural differences in conformity

Much of the work on conformity was conducted in the USA, but some has been done in other countries. P. Smith and M. Bond (1998) argue that whether conformity levels are 'high' or 'low' depends on the cultural context. For example, the 32 per cent conformity found by Asch may be considered high in the USA, where independence and individualism are valued. In a cross-cultural study by R. Shouval and colleagues (1975) they compared conformity to peer-group pressure between 12-year-old Israeli and Russian children, finding the Russian children (in a more collectivist society) much more conforming.

Smith and Bond compared conformity studies from several countries, noting that variations between them made direct comparison impossible. Some used Asch's design, others were similar to Crutchfield's, some used students as participants but others sampled from the general population or used unemployed people. However, there were some patterns in the levels of conformity found, namely:

- **Collectivist cultures** (where the importance of one's family, religion or race is paramount) produced higher levels than individualist cultures (where independence is most valued). For example, there was higher conformity in Japan than in France.
- **Common experiences** amongst participants (for example, Indian teachers in Fiji) showed high levels of conformity to their group. This was supported by research in Japan which indicated that people who were already known to each other showed higher levels of conformity than a group of strangers.
- **Students** generally showed lower levels of conformity.

Factors affecting levels of conformity

Why do people conform? As we have seen, research shows that a number of factors affect levels of conformity. These factors include:

- **Ambiguity** – Sherif, Asch and Crutchfield found higher levels of conformity when information is uncertain
- **Unfamiliarity** – Sistrunk and McDavid demonstrated that when not familiar with the situation, participants are more conforming
- **Unanimity** – when everyone else in the group agrees, the individual is more likely to conform, according to Asch and Crutchfield
- **Need for approval** – individuals with a strong need for approval from others are more likely to conform
- **Low self-esteem** – those with low self-esteem are also more likely to conform
- **Social norms** – in a culture which stresses social cohesion, the individual is more likely to conform
- **Group strength** – where there are strong links between members of a group, individuals will show higher levels of conformity.

M. Deutsch and H. Gerrard (1955) have proposed two types of social influence. When we are unsure about something we look to others for answers. This is informational social influence and is the type of influence occurring in the first two factors above ambiguity and unfamiliarity. On the other hand, when we conform because we want to be approved of or accepted by others, this is normative social influence.

Obedience

Obedience can be defined as:

- following a command, order or instruction which is given by an authority figure.

 This contrasts with **conformity**, because no-one asks or tells us to conform. Obedience is an important factor in society; we may obey orders because they benefit us or seem fair, but would we obey orders which were illegal, immoral or unjustified? One of the most widely-known psychological studies was carried out by Stanley Milgram who tried to answer this question.

Stanley Milgram's research

Milgram wanted to investigate whether Germans were particularly obedient to authority figures; this was a common explanation for the Nazi atrocities of the Second World War. He planned to test obedience first in an American setting before conducting research in Germany. Milgram (1963) selected **participants** by advertising for males between the ages of 20 and 50 years of age to take part in a study of learning at Yale University (a prestigious university in America).

The procedure was that the participant was paired with another person and they drew lots to find out who would be the 'learner' and who the 'teacher'. An experimenter took them into a room where the learner (who apparently had a mild heart condition) was strapped into a chair with electrodes attached to his arms (see Figure 1.4). The teacher and experimenter then went into an adjoining room which contained a shock generator with a row of switches marked from 15 volts ('slight shock') to 375 volts ('danger: severe shock') right up to 450 volts (see Figure 1.4).

The participant did not know that all of this was false: the 'learner' was a confederate, the drawing of lots was rigged so the participant was always the 'teacher', and the machine did not administer shocks. The participant was given a 45-volt shock (apparently from the machine) in order to make the procedure convincing.

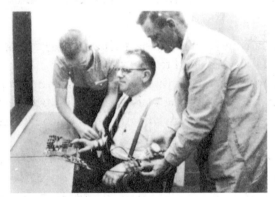

Figure 1.4 Milgram's 'learner' having the electrodes strapped on and the participant receiving a sample shock from the generator (from Milgram, 1974)

The participant/teacher was instructed to read out word pairs (such as 'blue' and 'girl') which the learner had to remember. The teacher was to give him an electric shock if he made a mistake or said nothing. If errors continued the shocks were to be increased. The learner started off quite well, but as he made more and more mistakes, the teacher had to increase the shocks. At 180 volts the learner shouted out that he could not stand the pain, at 300 volts he begged to be released, after 315 volts there was silence. Of course, this was all artificial.

Before starting, Milgram showed this description of the study to psychiatrists for their comments. They predicted, as did Milgram, that around 2 per cent would shock to the highest level but the majority would refuse to continue at a very early stage. However, all participants shocked to 300 volts and 65 per cent of participants continued to 450 volts. Despite this, participants showed considerable distress during the experiment. Three had seizures, several challenged the experimenter and asked if the learner could be checked. The experimenter responded with 'prods' such as 'Although the shocks are painful there is no permanent damage, so please go on' or 'You have no other choice, you must continue'.

Afterwards all the participants were **debriefed**. They were told what was really happening in the study and were introduced to the 'learner' so they could see that he was unharmed. They were assured that their own behaviour was normal. When Milgram followed up each participant several months later to ask their opinion and whether they had experienced any problems, he noted that 74 per cent said they had learned something of personal importance from the experiment.

Factors affecting levels of obedience

Milgram was astonished at these results, and continued his research by varying the basic procedure to discover what factors affected levels of obedience. The following factors were identified:

- **Surveillance** – if the experimenter left the room, the participants' obedience dropped to an average of 20 per cent who shocked to 450 volts.
- **Buffers** – this is anything that prevents those who obey from being aware of the full impact of their actions. In Milgram's design, the wall was a buffer between the teacher and the learner; when the learner was in the same room, obedience levels dropped to 40 per cent.
- **Prestige** – when the study was conducted in a run-down setting, fewer participants shocked to the maximum, so prestige of the setting increases obedience.
- **Authority** – Milgram proposed that when individuals perceive another to have legitimate authority over them, they no longer feel responsibility for their own actions; the individual becomes an agent of the authority. Milgram's experimenter wore a laboratory coat (a symbol of scientific expertise) and when participants protested, told them 'I'm responsible for what goes on here'. When the experimenter seemed to be an ordinary person, not wearing a laboratory coat, obedience was very low.
- **Personal responsibility** – when the participant had more direct responsibility for the suffering, such as putting the learner's hand on the electric plate, obedience dropped to 30 per cent. In contrast, when the participant instructed an *assistant* to press the switches, 95 per cent instructed to shock to 450 volts.
- **Disobedient models** – when participants were one of three 'teachers' and the others refused to give the shock, obedience dropped to 10 per cent. Several said afterwards that they had not realised they could refuse to continue.
- **Familiarity with the situation** – research by Rank and Jacobson (see p.14) suggests that lower levels of obedience occur if the participant is familiar with, and so more confident in, the situation.

Evaluation of Milgram's research

Participants in Milgram's studies could have walked out at any time: there were no harmful consequences (such as losing a job or being physically assaulted) if they did not obey. Milgram argued that this was a powerful (and unexpected) example of the human tendency to obey an authority figure, even when the demands are unreasonable. His studies created enormous interest and concern and have added to our understanding of human behaviour. Blind obedience would be reduced, argued Milgram, if people were aware of its dangers and were encouraged to question authority. His work contributes to that awareness.

Nevertheless, this research on obedience has generated many criticisms which chiefly relate to ethics, experimental validity and generalisation of results. Each of these is examined in turn below.

Ethics

Milgram's work is a vivid example of the importance of **ethics** in psychological research. It is valuable to compare the British Psychological Society's guidelines on ethics (see p.187) with the criticisms of Milgram's research which are listed below:

- **Distress** – participants were clearly caused distress, even suffering health risks. In the first series of experiments Milgram argued that he had no idea participants would show such a reaction; however, he still continued with this research even after he knew of the potential distress to participants.
- **Withdrawal** – despite evident distress, participants were not reminded that they could withdraw; in fact, when they protested they were told they had no choice but to continue.
- **Deception** – there was a large element of deception in the study. After debriefing, the great majority of participants said they were glad to have taken part. Milgram argued that this showed that the procedure was in fact acceptable.

When Milgram designed this experiment ethical constraints were not so restrictive, indeed his purpose in discussing his plans with psychiatrists was to obtain their opinions on what he planned to do. It is due to research such as this that psychologists have established ethical guidelines to protect participants.

Experimental validity – does the experiment actually test obedience?

Although some of the research which replicates Milgram's design does show very similar results, critics such as M. Orne and C. Holland (1968) argue that this is not a test of obedience, because **participants** did not believe what was happening in the experiment. The situation was absurd – participants were asked to shock someone, to death if necessary, because they could not remember that 'blue' was paired with 'girl'! Because of this unreality, participants suspended their own judgement and relied on the experts; indeed we saw earlier that when participants protested, the experimenter replied 'I'm responsible for what goes on here'.

Critics refer to **demand characteristics** (see p.180) – one of these is that participants obey the instructions of the experimenter. Hence the experiment does not show obedience to an authority figure, but conformity to experimental expectations. Although this is a persuasive argument, it is undermined by Hofling's research which is described in the next section.

It has also been argued that Milgram tested participants' trust in, not obedience to, authority. Obedience dropped when the experimenter left the room because the participant could not be sure that the researcher was still keeping an eye on things. When Milgram's study was replicated, but with participants who were led to believe that there was something a little odd about the experiment (in order to create distrust), levels of obedience were very low. Milgram himself noted that his participants came from a culture in which authority was trusted, but this was exactly the issue he was studying.

Can results be generalised to other situations?

Milgram's results cannot be generalised to real-life situations because there was **bias** in his sample of participants. They were **self-selected** (see p.193) and all were male, so the sample was not representative of the general population.

C. Hofling and colleagues (1966) studied obedience in a real-life setting by investigating whether nurses would knowingly break hospital rules in order to obey a doctor. A bottle of pills had been labelled 'Astroten' (see Figure 1.5) and placed in the ward medicine cabinet.

ASTROTEN
5 mg capsules
Usual dose: 5 mg
Maximum daily
dose: 10 mg

Figure 1.5 This is the label the nurses saw in the ward medicine cabinet

The nurse on duty received a phone call from a Dr Smith from the Psychiatric Department asking her to give his patient 20 mg of Astroten straight away. He explained that he was in a hurry and wanted the drug to have taken effect before he got to see the patient, and that he would sign the drug authorisation when he came on the ward in about ten minutes' time.

These instructions broke these hospital rules:

- nurses give drugs only after written authorisation
- nurses take instructions only from people they know
- maximum dosages should not be exceeded.

Nevertheless, 21 of the 22 nurses phoned by 'Dr Smith' obeyed the instructions, although someone stopped them from actually administering the drug, which was a harmless sugar pill. When interviewed afterwards, many nurses said that doctors frequently phoned instructions and became annoyed if the nurse protested. Half the nurses said they had not noticed what the maximum dosage was. The researchers described the situation to a **control group** of 21 nurses and then asked what they would have done. Each claimed that they would not have obeyed.

This disconcerting result was challenged in research by S. Rank and C. Jacobson (1977) using a similar procedure, but the drug was Valium®. Here only 2 of the 18 nurses obeyed the instructions, the researchers concluding that familiarity with the drug was one reason for the low level of obedience in their study.

The results of Hofling's hospital study echo Milgram's – people do not expect others to obey as often as they actually do. Although this study suggests that Milgram's results can be generalised to real-life situations, Rank and Jacobson's research suggests that familiarity with the situation is another factor which reduces levels of obedience.

 ## Cultural differences in obedience

As we noted above under Conformity, it is difficult to make direct comparisons between studies of obedience which have taken place in different countries. When experimental procedures are different, this may account for differences in results rather than differences in culture. Once again though, there seem to be some general patterns, for example:

- An Australian study by W. Kilham and L. Mann (1974) used students as male teachers and learners and female teachers and learners. Here there was 40 per cent obedience in males and 16 per cent in females. So where Milgram found no difference between males and females, the Australian research suggests that the sex of the victim, as well as the teacher, is a factor. An explanation for the overall lower levels of obedience is that there was a stronger tradition of criticising authority in Australia than in the USA, although the fact that the Australian study took place almost 15 years later could be a **confounding variable**.
- Research based on Milgram's procedure has shown greater than 80 per cent levels of obedience in Italy, Spain, Germany and Austria. Although procedures in each of these studies were not identical to Milgram's they did show consistently high levels.

● A different procedure was used in research by W. Meeus and Q. Raaijmakers (1986) in the Netherlands. They required participants to criticise a 'candidate' (actually a confederate) whom they were 'interviewing' for an important job. Here 92 per cent obeyed instructions, delivering the most insulting comments.

 As you may have noticed, most studies of obedience have taken place in the industrialised nations of the world, so although we are able to compare cultures, we are not comparing obedience in very different kinds of cultures.

The OCR exam

The OCR exam will test your ability to:

● define conformity and demonstrate some knowledge of research studies, e.g. the work of Asch
● define obedience and demonstrate some knowledge of research studies, e.g. the work of Milgram
● demonstrate knowledge of factors affecting levels of obedience and conformity
● evaluate the research on conformity and obedience including possible cultural differences.

Sample exam questions on social influence

1 What do psychologists mean by conformity?   (2 marks)
2 a Describe a research study on conformity.   (4 marks)
    b Give one criticism of the study.   (2 marks)
3 Describe one research study on obedience.   (4 marks)
4 Milgram's participants were a self-selected sample.   (1 mark)
    a Explain what is meant by this term.   (1 mark)
    b Explain its main advantage.   (2 marks)
5 Explain two factors or conditions which affect levels of obedience.   (2+2 marks)
6 Describe one ethical concern of Milgram's study.   (2 marks)
7 Explain the purpose of the control group of nurses in Hofling's
    study (p.14)   (3 marks)

Environment and Behaviour

Humans are social animals and being with others is crucial for us. However, we are not always comfortable with others; their presence may be intrusive or even threatening. This chapter discusses two of the methods we use to prevent the presence of other people from becoming unpleasant. These two, personal space and territoriality, enable us to regulate our interactions with other people. As you will see, we are able to do this in very subtle ways.

Personal space

E. Hall (1959) has described personal space as:

● an 'emotionally charged bubble of space which surrounds each individual'.

This invisible bubble is like a boundary which surrounds us and is carried with us when we move. If anyone crosses the boundary, they invade our personal space and we feel uncomfortable. Some environmental psychologists have proposed that personal space enables people to regulate their relationships with others, so personal space only has a meaning when two or more people are together.

We use our personal space as a buffer against others, which is why we feel discomfort if the space is invaded. When it is invaded we experience an emotional change which Hall described as unpleasant arousal. This arousal may create stress (see Stress and crowding on p.152–3), anxiety, fear or aggression. The size and shape of this invisible boundary varies depending on who we interact with. Hall (1966) used the term 'proxemics' for the study of space as a form of interpersonal communication. As a result of this research he identified four distances of personal space ranging from intimate to public. Details are shown in Table 2.1 below.

Personal space distance	Size of distance	Social use
Intimate distance	0 – 0.5 m	Used for an intimate relationship, as well as social circumstances such as shaking hands or sports such as wrestling.
Personal distance	0.5 – 1.5 m	Maintained by close friends and acquaintances and enables conversations to take place.
Social distance	1.5 – 4.0 m	For more formal situations, such as people who are acquaintances or in business transactions.
Public distance	Over 4.0 m	The distance between one person and a group, for example at a lecture, at a concert or political rally.

Table 2.1 Hall's personal space distances

Invasions of personal space

Invisible and unspoken assumptions form the basis of our interactions with others, and Harold Garfinkel tried to reveal these through his research. Personal space is an example; not only are we aware of our own and others' personal space, but we may make assumptions about people who invade that space. In one study Garfinkel (1964) asked students to bring their faces close to the face of an acquaintance whilst they were talking to them. These acquaintances showed confusion or embarrassment and several thought that the other person had sexual intentions because of their behaviour.

In 1966 N. Felipe and R. Sommer conducted two **field experiments** on personal space. One took place in the grounds of a large mental institution. When a man was sitting alone on a bench someone came and sat down next to him, sitting 15 cm away. If the participant moved along the bench the 'invader' followed. Observers noted the length of time before the participants left, and compared them with a **control group** (males sitting alone) who were watched from a distance. Results showed that 20 per cent had left after one minute (but none of the controls), and 50 per cent after nine minutes (8 per cent of the controls). The comparison of results for the two groups is shown in Figure 2. 1 on the next page.

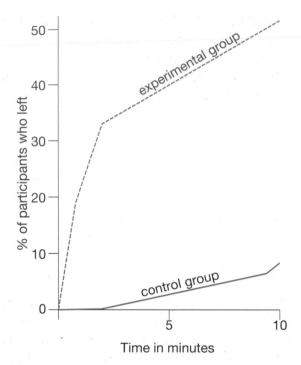

Figure 2.1 Graph showing length of time before Felipe and Sommer's participants fled

The second study by Felipe and Sommer took place in a library, using people who were sitting by themselves. Results showed that, when an 'invader' sat in the next chair and moved it closer, 70 per cent of participants had left their seats after 30 minutes, whereas only 13 per cent left when the participants allowed a gap of one chair between them.

GROUP ACTIVITY – Ethics in research

The type of procedure used in Garfinkel's or in Felipe and Sommer's research has been widely used to study personal space. Compare their procedure with the ethical guidelines on p.187 and as a group write up a critical evaluation of this work.

Evaluation of Felipe and Sommer's research

These studies were **field experiments**, so the participants' behaviour was natural as they were not aware they were taking part in an experiment. We can therefore assume that this is how people would behave if their personal space was invaded in real life. However, there are important weaknesses in this method and in the actual design of these studies, which we will consider now.

In a **field experiment** the researchers are unable to exert much control. They cannot, for example, find out why the participants left: it may have been completely unrelated to the presence of the invader. In addition, if only certain sorts of people are participants, then the sample is biased and the results cannot be **generalised** to the population at large. This was the case with Felipe and Sommer's studies because:

- They used only people who were sitting alone, and there may have been particular reasons why they were sitting alone in the mental institution.
- The type of people studying in a library may vary depending on the time of day.
- There were only male participants in the first study and, as we will see shortly, there are differences in the personal space of males and females.
- In the second study, the participants were all students and the invaders were young too. Results may have been different with people of different ages or if older people had 'invaded' younger people or *vice versa*.

 Ethically these studies contravened several guidelines (see pp.187–8). Invading a participant's personal space will have caused embarrassment and discomfort for most and possibly considerable **distress** to a few. As these were field experiments, it was not possible to gain **consent** nor to **debrief** participants, explain the purpose of the research or check on their wellbeing. In the library study, the invasion was likely to disrupt the student's concentration and perhaps halt their studying, all without the student's consent.

Ways of defending personal space

Felipe and Sommer's work showed that many participants changed the angle of the chair, pulled their elbows in and used books or other objects as barriers in order to defend their personal space. People also changed their body position, leaning away from the invader or turning the angle of the body to present more of a barrier. These barriers may indicate the size and shape of each person's space, as you will see below.

When we are unable to put up barriers or move away we simply try to maximise our personal space by making ourselves smaller – people in a crowded lift will stand up straight with their arms close by their sides and avoid eye contact with others.

Differences in personal space

You will notice from Table 2.1 that each of Hall's classifications covers quite a range. In others words, half a metre may be 'Intimate' for one person but

'Personal' for another. Research has shown that there is some pattern to these variations, in particular that men have a different personal space from women, and what is normal in one culture may be abnormal in another. We will look at these two types of difference now.

Gender differences

There are several differences between the personal space of men and women. When they are with another man, males generally maintain larger personal spaces than two females together. This could be because males tend to be more concerned about not being intimate with others of the same sex. However, another explanation for this difference is that females are generally fairly comfortable in intimate situations with other females.

Research also suggests that females have a smaller personal space when interacting with people they like, but a larger one with those they dislike. J. Aiello (1987) found that there does not seem to be this difference for men. Their personal space tends to be greater than women's but is similar for both liked *and* disliked people.

Some research has focused on *other* people's perception of personal space. For example, when a man stood 60 cm from a drinks fountain, fewer people came to use the fountain than when there was a woman standing in the same position.

Although we all have a personal space, it may not be shaped like a bubble. J. Fisher and D. Byrne's **field experiment** (1975) arranged for a confederate to invade the space of another person whilst they were sitting alone in a library. Invaders were either male or female, and sat next to the participant or opposite. After a few minutes the invader left, and a student (another confederate) then came over and asked for the participant's impressions. These were:

- **Male** participants disliked the invader who sat opposite, but did not mind when the invader sat by them.
- **Female** participants disliked the invader sitting next to them, but did not mind the invader sitting opposite.

Further research shows the same differences in the barriers people erect in a library, that is, men create more barriers than women when an invader sits opposite them, whereas women create more barriers when an invader sits at their side. These results suggest that our personal space is more like a flattened bubble; its shape depends on what sex we are.

GROUP ACTIVITY – How does the shape of personal space vary?

Each member of your group asks people, in an everyday setting, to stand in a clear space which you have marked by an X on the floor. You tell the person that you are going to approach them slowly and they must say when they feel that you are uncomfortably close. Approach each person from the four directions shown in Figure 2.2 and stop immediately you are told you are too close. Mark your stopping point on the floor.

When you have finished, thank the person for helping you and make sure you debrief them fully (see p.187). Measure the distance between each stopping point and the X mark, then draw the shape of each participant's 'personal bubble' on a piece of paper. Note the sex of the participant and the direction they were facing and pool your results with the rest of the group. Do you see a difference between the size and shape of each personal space? Is there a pattern in those differences?

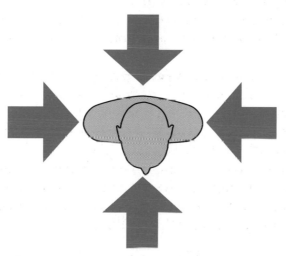

Figure 2.2 Four approaches for testing personal space

Cultural differences

Hall's classification of personal distance is based on studies in America, but he also conducted **cross-cultural** research on norms for interaction, looking at distance and the use of senses such as touch, eye contact and volume when speaking. He found that in cultures high in 'sensory contact' (such as French, Greek and Arabic) personal distances are much closer than in low 'sensory contact' cultures (such as American, English or Swiss). Because of these differences, someone standing too far away could cause offence in one culture, and standing too close could cause discomfort in another.

Figure 2.3 These men are very close together in this conversation. However, the listener would be feeling uncomfortable if he was from a culture which used a larger personal distance.

However, personal distances between members of sub-cultures appear to be more complex. As an example, research in the USA by J. Baxter (1970) showed that personal distances varied according to the setting. African-Americans interacted more closely in indoor settings, whereas Mexican-Americans were closest in outdoor settings.

Other research has highlighted differences in personal distance both between and within cultures. An explanation for this could be differences in status between members of the same culture. Status appears to be an important factor in interpersonal relations, and is discussed in relation to Prejudice on p.108.

Territoriality

Unlike personal space (which is portable and invisible), **territory** can be defined as:

- a physical area which is generally immovable and is owned or controlled by a person or group.

Territoriality is behaviour associated with the ownership or occupation of a space or area. By taking ownership, the individual claims it as their territory. For example, if you put your jacket on a desk when you leave the classroom, you are claiming ownership of that desk. The desk is your territory, even though it is only temporarily 'yours'.

Work on territoriality started with the study of animals, but increasingly this concept is being used to study human behaviour and to design environments which humans find agreeable. I. Altman and M. Chemers (1980) suggested three types of territory:

- **Primary territory** – this is an area over which we have relatively complete control and which is of central importance to us, such as a bedroom. Ownership of the territory is recognised by others and we would react strongly if this territory was invaded. Primary territory contributes to our sense of identity; for example, research on residents of old people's homes has shown that 'ownership' of a special chair in the public rooms is important for their personal identity.
- **Secondary territory** – is an area over which we have only partial control, perhaps for a short period of time (such as a table in a restaurant) or because we share it with others (such as a classroom). This has less importance to us.
- **Public territory** – is generally accessible to anyone and no one individual or group has a right to it. Examples include pavements, beaches and libraries. Public territory can be temporarily personalised with markers, for example by a person leaving a newspaper on a library chair while getting a book or setting up windbreaks on a beach (as in Figure 2.4).

Figure 2.4 Although the beach is public territory, some groups have personalised part of it using their windbreaks

Territory is important to humans, whether it is your bedroom, the 'land of your birth', your seat in the classroom or a space on the beach. Territory helps us to organise our behaviour and our interactions with others. For instance, someone reclaiming a beach ball from within the area of the windbreak would probably apologise, but would not do so if the ball was simply close to a group without a defined territory.

Many studies of territoriality have used the **observational method**. A typical example is the research by G. Haber (1980) who devised a **field experiment** which had 'invaders' sit in students' regular seats while the occupants were out of the classroom. When they returned, she observed that many of the students claimed ownership of their seats. The longer the seat had been occupied or the more marked it was with personal property, the more vigorous were the owner's efforts to reclaim it. The next time the class met, all the students who had been invaded arrived earlier and re-occupied *their* seats!

Ways of establishing and defending territory

As we have seen, humans have several ways of establishing and protecting territory. Some of these are:

- **Defining territory** – a key feature of territory is that it is a physical area which is defined. A chair or desk is clearly defined, but in an open space territory may be defined by walls, hedges, filing cabinets, furniture and so on. Research by E. Sundstrom and colleagues (1980) showed that office workers preferred to work in private offices (clearly defined territory) rather than an open-plan office. The windbreaks in Figure 2.4 temporarily define the group's territory.
- **Marking territory** – ownership of a territory may be publicised by markers. These could be personal possessions, a nameplate, national flag or graffiti. It appears that personal items such as a coat are more effective markers than neutral ones, such as a newspaper.
- **Defending territory** – markers may be an effective way of telling others to stay away, but sometimes territory may be actively defended against intruders, depending on its importance to the individual or group claiming ownership. Workers with their own office are able to shut the door, whereas those in open-plan offices have to use other tactics. One is for a person to face in to their territory so that their back is turned to the 'public' area, in effect providing a reminder that anyone who approaches is entering private territory. However, with larger territories, the opposite is more common. The individual takes a position which enables them to see and identify intruders and take action to deter them. An example of this is the idea of defensible space, which is examined in more detail below.

Defensible space

The term 'defensible space' refers to territory which is centred on the home. P. Bell and colleagues (1990) have defined **defensible space** as:

- a relatively stationary, bounded area which is home-centred and can be defended from intruders.

Defensible space is an important element in the design of homes, providing security against intrusion and crime. Figure 2.5 illustrates examples of homes with and without defensible space.

Figure 2.5 Homes with defensible space and homes without defensible space

Research suggests that crime is less likely to occur where there is a defensible space and residents reported feeling more secure. O. Newman (1972) compared the rate of crime in two New York housing projects. Brownsville was designed in small blocks built around a courtyard and housing five or six families, while Van Dyke consisted of high-rise buildings set a distance apart with parkland between. Although the same number of residents lived in both housing projects, the crime rate was 50 per cent higher in Van Dyke. Newman suggested that four factors were important in explaining the difference in crime rate. These were:

- **Zone of territorial influence** – this is defined by indicators that an area is private rather than public, such as flower pots or washing lines.
- **Opportunities for surveillance** – residents can easily see the common areas, so potential intruders can quickly be identified. Equally, the fact that an area is easy to survey will deter intruders. Windows and balconies should be designed to allow residents to overlook common areas.
- **Image** – the more anonymous a building is, the more public it seems, so names of residents and the personalisation of the property reduce anonymity.
- **Milieu** – the larger the space around a building, the more public it seems and the more likely it is to attract vandalism. Also, the more decayed the buildings, the higher the crime level.

Although buildings designed with defensible space are sometimes linked to lower crime levels, this is not always the case. There has been little research on how the elements of defensible space actually affect the social circumstances they are supposed to create. For example, window boxes and washing lines indicate a private area, but they also provide an opportunity for residents to chat and perhaps to strengthen community spirit. Until more is known about about how the elements of defensible space actually affect the residents, we are unable to explain why they may be more effective in reducing crime levels in some buildings rather than others.

Remembering the material in this chapter

As an aid to remembering the information in this chapter, it has been organised into a mind map (see Figure 2.6). This is a way of remembering information by linking it together visually. More details on memory aids such as this are described under 'Improving memory', pp.121–2.

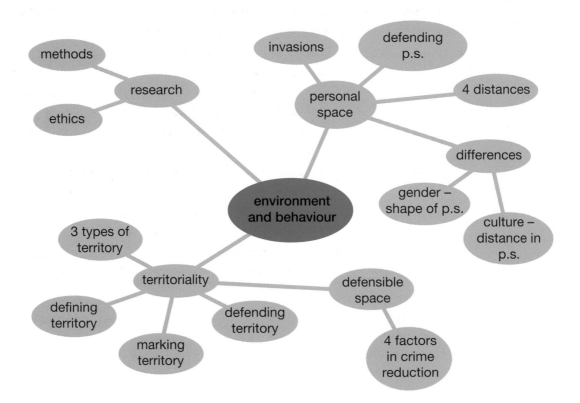

Figure 2.6   A mind map of the material on environment and behaviour

The OCR exam

The OCR exam will test your ability to:

● define the concept of personal space and demonstrate a knowledge of studies regarding the invasion of personal space, e.g. the work of Garfinkel or Felipe and Sommer
● consider possible cross-cultural and gender differences regarding personal space
● define territory as well as demonstrate a knowledge of different types of territory and the concept of defensible space, e.g. the work of Altman
● demonstrate knowledge of the ways in which an individual might establish and protect their personal space and territory, e.g. the work of Felipe and Sommer.

Sample exam questions on environment and behaviour

1 How do psychologists define the term territory?   (2 marks)
2 Identify one possible effect of the invasion of personal space.   (1 mark)
3 Describe one gender difference regarding personal space.   (2 marks)
4 What type of sampling method did Felipe and Sommer use?   (1 mark)
5 In environmental psychology what is meant by defensible space?   (2 marks)
6 Before carrying out a study, researchers need to consider ethical issues
   and possible solutions. Suggest solutions to the issues below: (2 marks)

Ethical issue	A solution
Right to withdraw	Participants must not be forced to continue in a study
Confidentiality	
Consent	

7 Describe and evaluate psychological research into how people
   establish and protect personal space and territory.   (12 marks)

Behavioural Psychology

Behavioural psychologists believe that psychology should focus on observable, overt behaviour and the processes by which that behaviour has been learned. This is illustrated in the next two chapters.

Chapter 3 explores Phobias and several ways of explaining what causes them. Chapter 4 considers Aggression, what causes it and whether there are cultural and gender differences in aggression.

Phobias

Why are some of us frightened of spiders, of the dark, of open spaces or of flying? According to behavioural psychologists, this fear is learned as a result of our experiences. In other words, we are not born with a fear of the dark, we learn to be frightened through the experiences we have. But equally, they argue that this fear can be unlearned, as a result of our experiences. As you will see in this chapter, the behaviourist explanation has its weaknesses, so we will also consider alternative explanations for these fears which, unlike the behaviourists, take human emotions and thinking into account.

What is a phobia?

A **phobia** can be defined as:

● an intense, persistent and irrational fear of something which is accompanied by a compelling desire to avoid and escape it.

This fear may be of a particular object (such as a spider), a situation (heights), a place (school) or an activity (flying). It may be so intense that it interferes with the individual's normal everyday functioning. Some of the more common phobias are listed in Table 3.1 on page 32.

Agoraphobia is the most common phobia for which people seek professional help, probably because it is the most restricting. It refers to the individual's fear that they will be overwhelmed by panicky feelings in a place where they feel exposed. These places are often public or open spaces. The description below may help you understand how an agoraphobic feels.

> ### A case of agoraphobia
>
> 'I remember the first time it happened, walking near my home suddenly everything seemed unfamiliar, I felt panic rising. I felt unreal, as though I didn't exist, I was sweating, my heart was pounding and my legs turned to jelly. I felt that if I took another step I would go over the edge into a dark pit. My only thought was that I must get home. Holding on to fences for support, I struggled home and collapsed crying.
>
> I couldn't go out for several days, but then I went out with my mother to visit my aunt, but again I felt panicky. I had shooting pains through my body and was sure I was going to die. My panic was uncontrollable, since then I can't go out alone. I live in constant fear of getting another attack.'

Nature of fear	Name of phobia
Fear of open spaces	Agoraphobia
Fear of embarrassing oneself in a social situation	Social phobia
Fear of spiders	Arachnophobia
Fear of confined spaces	Claustrophobia
Fear of heights	Acrophobia
Fear of foreigners	Xenophobia
Fear of school	School phobia

Table 3.1 Some of the more common phobias

Agoraphobia is one of the most difficult phobias to treat. Another is fear of flying, which often involves several fears. People who are phobic about flying report fear of confined spaces, of heights, of being out of control, or flying into 'nothing'. However, phobias related to specific objects, animals or places can be reduced by treatment. The reason for this may be related to the cause of the phobia, which is the main concern of this chapter.

Classical conditioning and phobias

A phobia is an irrational fear and, according to the principles of classical conditioning, the phobia is learned because fear has become associated with a particular object or experience. We will start by looking at how this association develops according to the principles of **classical conditioning**.

The principles of classical conditioning

If you heard a loud, unexpected noise, you would probably jump, your heart rate would increase, and other physiological responses would occur. All are part of the fear response (see Stress – the alarm reaction, p.144). Your 'jump' is an automatic response because you have no control over it. This automatic response is called an unconditioned response (UCR) because it does not have to be learned. The cause of this response (the loud noise) is called the unconditioned stimulus (UCS).

According to the principles of classical conditioning, you can learn to 'jump' in response to an entirely different stimulus. How does this learning occur? When the stimulus which made you jump (the loud noise) is presented at the same time as a *different* stimulus, you learn to associate them.

The principles of classical conditioning were first identified by Ivan Pavlov, a Russian physiologist, who was studying digestion in dogs in the early 1900s. While he was measuring how much saliva the dogs produced in different circumstances, he noted that they began salivating when they heard the researcher's footsteps approaching.

Salivation occurs automatically when an animal smells food, but Pavlov reasoned that the dogs in his study had learned to associate the sound of footsteps with the arrival of food because the two stimuli (footsteps and food) had occurred together so many times.

Pavlov tested this learning with the apparatus shown in Figure 3.1. The dog did not salivate on seeing the empty bowl but did so when food was in the bowl. After presenting food in the bowl on many occasions, the dog eventually learned to salivate even when the bowl was empty.

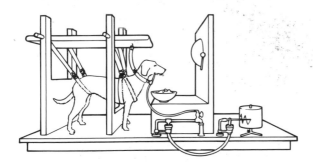

Figure 3.1 Pavlov's apparatus for studying conditioning with dogs

There are some special terms to describe this learning. To begin with, salivation (the **unconditioned response**) occurred with the presence of food (the **unconditioned stimulus**). After pairing together the bowl and the food many times, salivation had become conditioned to an empty bowl. This empty bowl is therefore the **conditioned stimulus**, and salivation is now called the **conditioned response** because it occurs with the conditioned stimulus.

The case of Little Albert

An example of this learning is well-illustrated by Little Albert. In research which has been heavily criticised, J. Watson and R. Rayner (1920) created a phobia in this healthy 11-month-old boy using classical conditioning. Whilst he was happily playing, a steel bar just behind him was struck with a hammer. He showed the fear response to the loud noise – he was startled and began to cry. Fear is an **unconditioned response** because it is automatic: no learning is required. However, the little boy did not show the fear response when he was given various objects, such as a white rat, a rabbit or cotton wool.

Little Albert was then given the white rat and whilst playing with it the steel bar was struck, he was startled and began to cry. After a few more trials in which the **unconditioned stimulus** (the noise) was made whilst he was playing with the white rat, Albert cried as soon as he saw the white rat and tried to crawl away. His fear had become conditioned to a new stimulus, the white rat.

The stimulus may be all kinds of things, such as an object, a person or a situation. By itself it has no effect on the individual, it is neutral. However, once it causes the response, as the white rat eventually triggered a response in Little Albert, it is called the **conditioned stimulus** (CS) because the person has become conditioned to it. Also, because the response is now given to the *conditioned* stimulus, it is called the **conditioned response** (CR). Table 3.2 sets out the process of classical conditioning.

	Stimulus	Response
Before conditioning starts	White rat	No fear response
Before conditioning starts	Loud noise (UCS)	Fear response (UCR)
During trials	Loud noise + White rat	Fear response
When conditioning has occurred	White rat (CS)	Fear response (CR)

Table 3.2 The process of classical conditioning

Generalisation and extinction

If a slightly different conditioned stimulus is presented and the conditioned response still occurs, then the response has been generalised to another stimulus. Watson and Rayner found that similar stimuli, for example a rabbit or cotton wool, also created the fear response in Little Albert. His fear of the white rat had become **generalised** to other similar objects.

The learned response can also be unlearned, which is known as **extinction**. Watson and Rayner planned to use extinction in order to rid Albert of his fear. To do this they would have given him the rat to play with, but there would be no loud noise. In other words, the conditioned stimulus is presented without the unconditioned stimulus. Gradually the conditioned response no longer occurs, and finally Little Albert would show no fear response to the white rat. Unfortunately the little boy was taken away before this could be done.

Evaluation of Watson and Rayner's research

Despite their intention to extinguish Little Albert's fear response, Watson and Rayner's conduct as researchers was unethical as they clearly caused the child distress and psychological harm. In addition, there was already evidence that extinction may not have eliminated his fear response because Pavlov and others found that with animals whose responses had been extinguished, after some delay, the animal could once again show the response when presented with the conditioned stimulus. This is called **spontaneous recovery**. So even if Watson and Rayner had extinguished Little Albert's fear response immediately after the experiment, he may have shown it weeks later if he encountered a white furry animal or cotton wool.

Operant conditioning and phobias

According to the principles of operant conditioning, we learn because of the consequences of our actions. If we do something that brings pleasant consequences, then we are likely to do it again. The behaviour has been reinforced by its consequences. There are two types of **reinforcement** – positive and negative.

On the other hand, if our actions bring unpleasant consequences we are *less* likely to repeat them. Here the behaviour has been weakened because of its consequences, which is called **punishment**. We will explore these ideas in more detail now, whilst considering how they may explain phobias.

Positive reinforcement

When a behaviour brings consequences which are pleasant for the individual, then he or she is likely to repeat the behaviour. As an example, a small child may be a little frightened of the dark, so, to reassure him, his mother gives extra cuddles. This is pleasant for the child, and if his mother starts to give less comfort he may show greater fear in order to maintain the comfort he has been getting. Thus, because his mother **reinforces** his show of fear, his fearful behaviour increases and eventually a phobia may be created.

Negative reinforcement

Behaviour can also be strengthened by negative reinforcement, but this is because the behaviour stops something unpleasant. Negative reinforcement can provide an explanation for school phobia. When a child is unhappy at school, for whatever reasons, then going to school is unpleasant. If the child stays away from school, then the unpleasant experience is avoided, so the child is even more likely to want to stay away from school, and may thus develop school phobia. Because staying away *stops* the unpleasant experience of school, this is called **negative reinforcement**.

Avoidance learning

In the example above, the child avoids school and thus his fear is reduced. This is called **avoidance learning** because the child has learned to avoid the unpleasantness. However, the fear of school is still present in the child, and the only way to unlearn the fear is in fact to have contact with the feared situation – being at school. This is one of the reasons why it may be difficult to treat phobias, to **extinguish** them.

If you find the photograph in Figure 3.3 unpleasant, then you will probably avoid spiders whenever you can. However, parents who fear spiders may want to

Figure 3.2 How fearful do you find this photograph?

hide this fear from their children. As a result they *have* to be exposed to spiders, they cannot always avoid them. Gradually the parent's fear may be reduced.

Punishment

Punishment is anything which weakens behaviour. It does so because the consequence of an action is unpleasant for the individual. Imagine someone who feels very self-conscious and lacking in confidence when they are amongst other people. Being in a social situation makes them anxious and embarrassed. Someone like this finds that their action (going into a social situation) brings unpleasant consequences (**punishment**) for them. They become less inclined to mix with other people and so a fear of social situations develops.

An evaluation of classical and operant conditioning

If we compare classical with operant conditioning, we can see both similarities and differences. Similarities are that:

- Learning takes place through association between two events. In classical conditioning it is the pairing of the unconditioned and conditioned stimulus, and in operant conditioning it is the pairing of the behaviour with reinforcement or punishment.
- The learned behaviour becomes stronger if these pairings are repeated.
- Generalisation, discrimination and extinction occur in both types of learning.

The differences between classical and operant conditioning are summarised in Table 3.3.

	Classical conditioning	Operant conditioning
What behaviour can be conditioned?	Reflexive/automatic	Random/voluntary
Why does learning occur?	Two stimuli have been presented together	Because of consequences of behaviour
How certain is behaviour?	Stimulus always produces response	Behaviour probable but not certain
Can new behaviour be created?	No	Yes

Table 3.3 Differences between classical and operant conditioning

Classical and operant conditioning are examples of the behaviourist approach, which was hugely influential in psychology in the middle of the last century. Some of the advantages of this approach are:

- it focuses on what is observable and measurable, so it enables psychologists to measure the phobic's behaviour and check if treatment is effective.
- it helped establish the credibility of psychology as a serious scientific discipline, so that classical and operant conditioning methods have successfully been used to treat phobias.

However, this approach has been criticised on a number of points, some of the most important being:

- classical conditioning assumes all phobics have had a terrifying experience when encountering the object or situation about which they are phobic. Operant conditioning predicts that the consequences of the behaviour will create the phobia. If this is so, why are so many people frightened of things they have no previous experience of?
- conditioning fails to explain why people are often fearful of the same things, such as snakes or spiders or heights.
- behaviourism fails to take account of human emotions and of cognitive abilities – to reason, to justify, to understand, to discuss.

GROUP ACTIVITY – Researching phobias on the Internet

Using the Internet, try to find the following information (tip: use search words such as phobia, agoraphobia, anxiety disorders, mental health):

1 Name one phobia that has not been mentioned in this chapter.
2 You will see a number of suggestions for treatment of phobias; one is CBT. What does CBT stand for?
3 Name one drug that can be used to help treat a phobia, and say what effect the drug is supposed to have.

Alternative explanations for phobias

Some of the weaknesses noted above are addressed by alternative explanations for phobias, three of which we consider now.

Preparedness

An explanation why people are more phobic of spiders than, for example, cars (which are much more dangerous) is that there is an innate element to such fears. M. Seligman (1971) proposed that our ancestors were threatened by many dangers, and being sensitive to these dangers would increase their chance of survival – as a result, we have evolved the ability to associate certain stimuli with danger and this ability (or preparedness) explains phobias to things (snakes) or situations (heights) which may be dangerous. The notion of preparedness therefore explains why many people are fearful of the same things and of situations they have no direct experience of. Conditioning theories cannot explain these points.

Social learning theory and phobias

According to the principles of social learning theory, phobias are learned from observation of other people. A detailed description of social learning theory is given in Chapter 4, but the key features are observation, imitation and reinforcement. Let us consider how they might explain arachnophobia – a fear of spiders:

- **Observation** – a child watches her older brother's behaviour when he finds a spider in the bath. He runs out of the bathroom, screaming and shaking. His mother consoles him until he is calm and reassured.
- **Imitation** – the little girl sees a spider and imitates the behaviour of her brother. He acts as a model because he is similar, more powerful and was reinforced for his behaviour by his mother's actions.
- **Reinforcement** – when the little girl copies her brother's actions, she is consoled by her mother.

 In contrast with conditioning theories, social learning theory can explain why phobias occur in people with no direct contact with the feared object or situation – they develop through observation of others. Like operant conditioning, reinforcement plays a key role in this explanation, but it is not as successful as classical conditioning at reducing phobias because seeing other people behave fearlessly when confronted by spiders, heights or open spaces does not seem to help the phobic.

Social learning theory can explain how phobias develop in children but as it incorporates human abilities to remember, to reason and be self aware, it is less successful in explaining phobias in adults, which conditioning theories can explain.

Psychoanalytic theory and phobias

Sigmund Freud proposed that our behaviour is caused by unconscious forces. These are the basis of the individual's personality, which is made up of three parts:

- The **id** contains the instinctive sexual and aggressive energies that we are born with, and these instincts are buried in our unconscious. When a need arises we are driven to satisfy it immediately.
- The **ego** starts developing at around three years old, as we begin to understand that we cannot always have what we want and must satisfy our needs in realistic ways. For example, we cannot show our true feelings towards our parents.
- The **superego** develops at around six years of age and is the moral part of our personality which is also in the unconscious.

The role of the ego is to mediate the conflict between the urgent demands of the selfish id and the restraints of the superego. We are not aware of this conflict because it occurs in the unconscious, but we *are* aware of the anxiety it creates.

The ego must handle this anxiety but if it threatens to overwhelm the ego we protect it by using **ego defence mechanisms**. Three which relate to phobias are:

- **Repression** – in which we force memories of distress or conflict into our unconscious, where they remain unresolved. For example, an explanation for agoraphobia (the fear of open spaces) may be that the individual was left alone as a small child. The distress this caused has been **repressed**, but nevertheless the anxiety enters consciousness when he or she has to enter a situation where they feel exposed, vulnerable and alone.
- **Displacement** – in which we transfer our negative feelings (such as aggression, jealousy, fear) away from the cause of the feelings and onto something which will not harm us. For example, a psychoanalytic explanation for xenophobia could be that an individual hated his father and was frightened of him. He was unable to express these feelings towards the father, and so **displaced** them on to foreigners (see The authoritarian personality, p.102). The individual feels able to express his feelings towards foreigners in a way that he cannot towards his father.
- **Projection** – in which unacceptable feelings are attributed to someone else. Another explanation for xenophobia is that a man who hated his father (and unconsciously wanted to harm him) might **project** these feelings on to foreigners. He sees foreigners as wanting to harm him and is therefore fearful of them.

Phobics experience powerful emotions which Freud's theory can explain but conditioning theories ignore the emotional experience. This theory can also explain why the phobic is fearful of objects or situations with which they have no direct experience. However, because conflicts are in the unconscious, they are not accessible, so it is not possible to be sure that these are the causes of phobias. Psychoanalytic theory also fails to explain why many people who experienced being left alone or were frightened of their father do not have phobias.

GROUP ACTIVITY – Explaining agoraphobia

Read the agoraphobic's account on p.32. In pairs, answer the following questions and then compare your answers with other pairs.

1   What aspect of the above description can be explained by operant conditioning? Why?
2   What aspect cannot be explained by operant conditioning? Are any of the three alternative explanations more appropriate? Why?

The OCR exam

The OCR exam will test your ability to:

● demonstrate an understanding of the basic principles of classical conditioning and operant conditioning
● give a definition of a phobia and be aware of some of the more common phobias
● understand the possible role of classical and operant conditioning in phobias, e.g. the case of Little Albert
● be aware of the limitations of the classical and operant conditioning explanations, e.g. alternative causes.

Sample exam questions on phobias

1   Describe what is meant by a 'conditioned response' in psychology.   (2 marks)
2   Explain the effect of negative reinforcement.   (2 marks)
3   Describe what is meant by a phobia.   (2 marks)
4   Identify two examples of a phobia.   (1+1 mark)
5   Outline one ethical concern about the case of Little Albert.   (2 marks)
6   a Identify one limitation of the classical and operant
        conditioning explanations.   (1 mark)
    b Outline an alternative cause for phobias.   (2 marks)

Aggression

Although most of us recognise aggression when we see it, providing an adequate definition of it is difficult. One common distinction is that made between instrumental and hostile aggression. Instrumental aggression is used to achieve a specific goal, perhaps to protect yourself or to get your own way; it is not necessarily accompanied by anger. Hostile aggression is aimed purely at damaging someone or something, and is often done in anger. In this chapter we will focus on how social learning theory explains human aggression, and then evaluate this theory whilst considering some alternative explanations.

Social learning theory and aggression

Social learning theory proposes that we learn not simply by **reinforcement**, but also by observing other people and imitating their behaviour, which is why it is also called observational learning. Albert Bandura's studies of aggression form the basis for the principles of social learning, as you can see below.

Observation

We frequently watch other people, and children in particular observe others a great deal of the time. When they are observing others, they notice what they do and how they do it, what they say and how they say it. They notice how other people respond to what is said or done, so they observe the consequences of other people's behaviour.

Models

In social learning theory, anyone whose behaviour is observed like this is called a **model**. The type of people who are more likely to be models are those who are:

- **Similar to the child** – such as someone of the same sex, same age, same family or with the same interests.
- **Powerful** – such as a parent, teacher, pop star, sports star, cartoon hero or heroine.
- **Caring** – such as a parent or teacher.
- **Reinforced** – if the child sees that the model's behaviour leads to pleasant consequences (such as gaining approval), it is called **vicarious reinforcement** because the observer is reinforced indirectly.

Imitation

If the observer imitates the behaviour we know that the behaviour has been learned. For example, a boy might punch his teddy-bear in the same way as the hero in a cartoon punched another character. The child may say the same things or imitate the noises which accompanied the punch. If other characters in the cartoon showed admiration for this action, the child is even more likely to copy the hero's behaviour. This would be an example of vicarious reinforcement.

However, you can see from Bandura's research (described below) that even though the behaviour has been learned, it is not necessarily performed.

Reinforcement

The individual is more likely to perform the behaviour again if they are rewarded for doing so. The reward acts as reinforcement (see p.35 on Phobias). If the boy punches like the cartoon character and wins admiration from his friends, this is **reinforcement** and he is likely to continue. However, he is less likely to do it at home if his parents disapprove of his behaviour, as their disapproval acts as **punishment**. In this way the individual learns to behave in different ways, depending on the circumstances, because they have learned that the same behaviour brings different consequences in different circumstances.

Bandura's research on aggression

Albert Bandura conducted a series of **laboratory experiments** which studied the effect on children of watching an adult behave aggressively. For instance, Bandura and colleagues (1961) arranged for an adult to hit and kick a large inflatable doll (called a Bobo doll) whilst a child was in the room. Afterwards the child had the opportunity to play with a range of toys, including the doll, whilst the adult was present.

Bandura changed this procedure in later experiments, because in the **experimental condition** he showed children a *film* of someone being aggressive to the doll. Children in the **control condition** watched a non-violent film.

Whilst each of the children were playing afterwards they were **observed** through a one-way mirror, and the number of incidents of aggression was noted. A summary of the main findings is given below:

- Higher levels of aggression were recorded in participants who had seen a model of the same sex.
- Boys performed more acts of aggression than girls.
- Comments from the children indicated their awareness of what was appropriate behaviour, as some said 'Ladies shouldn't do things like that'.
- Children who had seen the model punished after being aggressive showed lower levels of aggression than those who saw the model rewarded.
- When participants were asked to reproduce as much of the model's behaviour as they could remember, the majority were able to do so accurately regardless of whether the model had been reinforced or punished. Some children had not previously been aggressive towards the doll when they had the chance, even though they could do so accurately when asked. These children had *learned* the behaviour even though they did not imitate it.

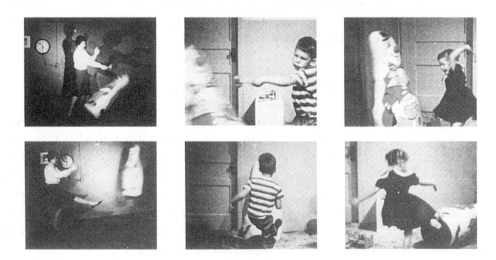

Figure 4.1 Here you can see the aggressive behaviour of the female model and the subsequent behaviour of a boy and girl who watched the model (from A. Bandura *et al.*, 1961)

An evaluation of Bandura's research on aggression

The advantages of this research are that results provided evidence for the principles of social learning theory, which is an important explanation for a range of human behaviours, including aggression, moral development, gender and phobias. Bandura and his colleagues showed how children learned new behaviours, and that these could be learned even without reinforcement. They also demonstrated how much the media can influence children's behaviour.

Despite this, there are several weaknesses in the research, such as:

- Bandura's results over-stressed the power of models, because of the **demand characteristics** of the situation. The children may have thought that they were supposed to copy the behaviour of the adult when they saw the same toys afterwards. Research has shown that in real-life situations with other humans (rather than inflatable dolls), children showed much lower levels of aggression.
- There are ethical concerns about Bandura's research; he taught children how to be aggressive and this may have caused problems for them later if they imitated the adult's behaviour. Children may have been **distressed** to see an adult behaving aggressively, particularly a female. Those children who had not been aggressive towards the doll may have been constrained by their own thoughts of what is right and wrong (morality), but Bandura's encouragement to behave aggressively suggested that it was permissible to do this.
- Bandura failed to distinguish between aggression and play fighting. Research by Cumberbatch (1990) found that children who had not seen the inflatable doll before were five times more likely to imitate aggressive behaviour against it than children who had played with it before. This suggests that higher levels of aggression were related to the novelty value of the toy.

The role of the media in aggression

Bandura's research showed that children could learn new ways of being aggressive from their observation of models. This raised the question of what role the media might play in encouraging aggression and violence in society. The presentation of aggression and violence in films, cartoons, TV programmes, computer games and books provides models which children and adults may imitate. As a result of concern over this, there was a rapid increase in research to discover more about the level and type of violence shown in the media, and to look at what role the media's presentation of violence might play in aggressive behaviour.

Research on the role of the media

In a **natural experiment** by T. Williams and colleagues (1986), the children in three Canadian towns were compared to discover whether television had an influence on their levels of aggression. At the start of the study, one town had no television reception (they called it 'Notel'), another town had one channel ('Unitel') and a third had several channels ('Multitel'). A year later Notel had one channel, Unitel had two channels.

The researchers obtained measures of the children's levels of aggression before additional channels were received and again one year afterwards. They **observed** the children in playgrounds, and asked teachers and children to rate aggression. As you can see from Figure 4.2, results showed that aggression (verbal and physical) increased after Notel children began watching TV, and this was true for both boys and girls. In addition Williams, found a **positive correlation** between the amount of time a child watched TV and the amount of aggression he or she showed.

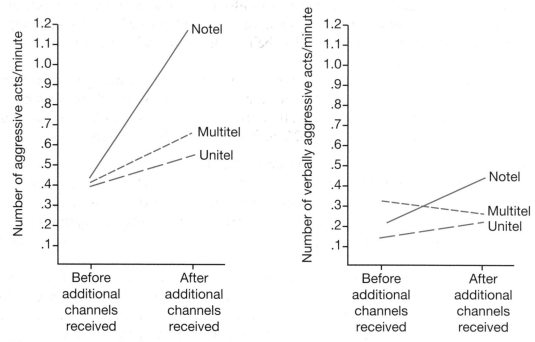

Figure 4.2 Results from a study of TV and aggression

There are two points to be made about these results:

- A correlation does not mean that time watching TV causes aggression, or that aggression makes children watch TV more, only that these two variables are related, they occur together.
- The children in all three towns showed similar levels of aggression when the study started, despite different experiences of TV. It could be that the Notel children's

aggression levels began to fall after the researchers left, bringing them closer to their original level.

Research which showed that children's aggression was related to the amount of violent television they watched, and that this relationship was apparent when they became adult, was provided by L. Eron (1972). He found this positive correlation in eight-year-old boys and the same children at 18 years old.

Rather than use the correlational method, some psychologists use the **experimental method** in order to test cause and effect. In laboratory experiments, for example, one group is exposed to a violent film and the other to a non-violent film. The level of aggression shown by the participants in each group is then observed. Typically levels are higher in those who watched the violent film.

In **field experiments**, already-established groups are exposed to violent programmes and tested before and afterwards for their aggression and hostility. Although the setting is more natural, because the groups are already established the researchers cannot assign participants **randomly** to groups. In addition, behaviour may be affected because the participants are in an established group – so **group norms** and peer pressures may affect behaviour. As individuals, people may not behave in the same way.

Overall then, there is conflicting evidence that media violence (particularly in television programmes) causes aggression in viewers. However, there is stronger evidence that there is a correlation between the two. How might this be explained in terms of social learning theory? The following may be of interest:

● **Imitation** – media violence offers models, which children or adults may copy. There is evidence of 'copycat' crimes occurring after highly publicised crimes on television or in films. Not only are aggressive acts modelled, but also the ways in which aggression can be used. For example, the viewer may see aggression as a way of solving conflicts, of getting your own way, of how to treat people who are weaker.

● **Models** – we are more likely to copy those who are similar or powerful. This could help to explain the correlation between an individual's level of aggression and their preference for watching violent television programmes. That is, people who have higher levels of aggression see aggressive characters as similar to themselves and are therefore more likely to use them as models. Aggressive characters in the media are often powerful, they dominate others or save the world through violence. Social learning theory proposes that those who are seen to be powerful will be used as models.

● **Reinforcement** – despite seeing violence in the media, people know that in general society disapproves of violence. This disapproval should act as **punishment** and so weaken violent behaviour when it is shown. However, if the individual finds aggression or violence brings pleasant consequences, then they are more likely to continue such behaviour. Examples of pleasant consequences are getting ownership of something, getting your own way, winning approval from your peers, releasing pent-up anger, getting attention from adults.

Eight-year-olds play at war

The site of the old Smithsons factory has become a battle-ground for children as young as 8 years old. The youngsters cover the lower part of their faces with scarves and hurl stones at each other, using the partly demolished walls as protection.

The parent of one child, who was cut on the head by a stone, said 'There is nothing for these kids to do here. This place looks like a war zone and the kids are bored, so they just copy what they see on the TV.'

Mike, at 14 years old, is one of the leaders. He says

Figure 4.3 Although social learning theory can explain the behaviour of these youngsters, are any of the other explanations in this chapter useful?

Is violence on television increasing?

One way to answer this question is to use the research method called **content analysis** (see p.178). Researchers studying violence on television first have to define what they consider to be violent or aggressive acts and then count their frequency in various programmes. An example is the research by G. Cumberbatch (1987), which analysed the output of the four terrestrial channels over four separate weeks in 1986. Cumberbatch found that 30 per cent of programmes contained some violence, averaging 1.14 violent acts per programme. These figures included boxing and wrestling, but if verbal threats were included the rate of violent acts per programme increased.

A decade later, similar research which included satellite channels found that on these channels the number of violent acts per hour was approximately twice that of the terrestrial channels. However, the overall conclusion by researchers was that the increase in violence in society was greater than the increase in violence on television.

An evaluation of social learning theory

You can see that according to social learning theory, learning occurs spontaneously, it does not have to be reinforced. A strength of the theory is the importance it places on the social environment. It focuses on each individual as a model for the behaviour of others, and highlights the role of parents, teachers, celebrities, sports stars and the media in providing models of aggressive and non-aggressive behaviour.

Another strength is that it includes both behaviourist and cognitive elements in its explanation. Whereas behaviourists claimed that learning could be explained without taking account of mental activities, social learning theorists argue that the mind mediates, in the sense that, for example, we imitate a behaviour when we have seen it bring pleasant consequences for others, or we learn a behaviour but may not perform it if we think it is inappropriate. We also use cognitive functions, such as perception and memory, in order to observe and reproduce behaviour.

One weakness of the theory is that it proposes aggressive behaviour is simply learned by observation, rather than being caused by something. We know from our own experiences and observations that aggression often seems to have a cause. Other explanations for aggression focus on causes, and these include biological causes, an innate drive to aggress, and the role of frustration. We will look at these explanations in more detail now.

Alternative explanations for aggression

The previous explanation for aggression represents the social and behavioural approach in psychology, and in doing so it excludes biological factors. The next three explanations look at biological causes, at Freud's theory of an innate drive to aggress and at how this may be linked with frustration in the frustration–aggression hypothesis.

The biological explanation

This explanation includes the role of the brain, of hormones and chemicals in aggression. The higher levels of aggression shown by males, for example, has been linked to higher levels of the hormone testosterone (see p.159 on Sex and Gender). Research has identified higher levels of testosterone in violent rather than non-violent criminals, but higher levels also in dominant but non-violent criminals. This suggests that the relationship between aggression and testosterone is complex.

An extreme example of the role of biology comes from the case of Charles Whitman. He shot his mother, his wife and then more than a dozen students in the University of Texas in 1966, before being killed by police.

Prior to this he had sought help for the overwhelming violent impulses he was experiencing and asked that an autopsy be performed on him after his death to see if there was any physical disorder. Subsequently he was found to have had a tumour in a part of the brain related to aggression – the temporal lobe.

Psychoanalytic theory and aggression

Sigmund Freud proposed that humans are born with an instinct for self-destruction, which he called **thanatos**. Aggression is the drive that enables us to satisfy this instinct. The aggressive urges are constantly building up within us, and have to be released in order to prevent a sudden explosion of aggression. Our death instinct conflicts with our life instinct (called the **libido**), yet both of these instincts are constantly in need of satisfaction. The libido and thanatos are part of the **id**, which we looked at along with the **ego** and **superego**, under Phobias (see p.40).

Freud proposed that the **ego** (the part of our personality which tries to satisfy our instincts in a realistic way) manages these conflicting instincts and avoids self-destruction by directing our self-destructive energy outwards. However, we need to do this in a way that meets the demands of our superego, which is the moral part of personality, so we use:

- **sublimation** – channelling aggression into acceptable activities such as sport
- **displacement** – transferring aggression outwards onto someone or something else
- **catharsis** – releasing aggression by watching someone else be aggressive.

Freud called these methods **ego defence mechanisms**.

Evaluation of the psychoanalytic explanation for aggression

Many aspects of Freud's theory are difficult to test because they are so abstract: for example, the id, superego and displacement. However, research has failed to support Freud's predictions that using the ego defence mechanisms would release (and therefore reduce) our pent-up aggression.

Critics argue that there is little evidence that watching or participating in competitive sport reduces aggression; indeed, research suggests that it increases aggression. This finding is better explained by social learning theory than by Freud's explanation.

Nevertheless, the concept of aggression as an instinctive drive is a powerful one, and has been developed into the explanation we turn to next.

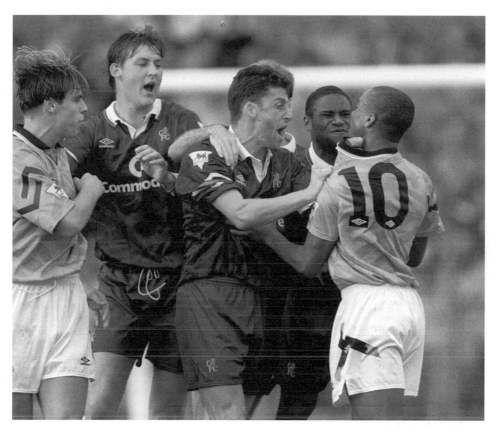

Figure 4.4 Watching sport should reduce aggression according to Freud

The frustration–aggression hypothesis

In their explanation, J. Dollard and colleagues (1939) also used the idea of aggression as a drive which has to find an outlet, but they proposed that this drive is frustration. They linked this view to learning theory, saying the frustration is the stimulus and aggression is the response. Frustration occurs when we are unable to achieve a goal, whether it is getting the job we want, finishing a task on time, making someone listen to us or getting the DVD player to work. Failure to achieve a goal creates frustration, which always leads to aggression, according to Dollard. This aggression may be released towards the cause of frustration, or be displaced on to others.

Evaluation of the frustration–aggression hypothesis

Although the frustration–aggression hypothesis incorporates both the stimulus–response ideas of learning theory and Freud's idea of an innate aggressive drive, it has been widely criticized for presenting a simplistic explanation.

For example, a boxer is aggressive but not necessarily frustrated, someone who is unable to find a job may be frustrated but be withdrawn and depressed rather than aggressive. One critic was N. Miller (1941) who proposed that frustration *may* lead to a variety of responses, depending on factors such as fear of retaliation and the reasons for frustration. The following factors affect the frustration we experience:

- how close we are to reaching our goal
- whether the frustrating event is due to chance or intention
- the number and intensity of frustrations that occur together
- our emotional state.

Another weakness of the frustration–aggression hypothesis is that it cannot explain why aggression occurs without frustration. For example, people imitate others' behaviour (social learning theory) or aggress because others in their group do (conformity). Critics such as L. Berkowitz (1968) argued that frustration does not cause aggression directly, but does arouse anger which in turn creates a readiness to act aggressively. He proposes that this readiness to act will be triggered if the individual sees aggressive cues such as weapons or others being aggressive.

Differences in levels of aggression

Research indicates that males show higher levels of aggression than females, and that aggression levels vary both between cultures and within cultures. Let us examine some of the evidence.

Gender differences

Research consistently shows that boys show higher levels of aggression overall than girls. This pattern is evident in countries as different as Mexico, Ethiopia and Switzerland. Some examples of this research are:

- J. Langlois (1980) studied pairs of children playing in a well-stocked playroom; observers noted the behaviour of same-sex pairs and boy-girl pairs. Results showed little difference in levels of aggression at three years old. By five years old, however, boys consistently showed more aggression than girls – but only towards other boys. This finding is a reflection of Bandura's work (described on pp.43–4), where children commented that aggressive behaviour was not 'ladylike'.
- A study of 10–12-year-olds showed that children differ in their attitudes to aggressive children: aggressive boys got more attention than non-aggressive boys and were more liked by their peers. This is an example of boys rewarding their peers for aggressive behaviour. Aggressive girls were not liked by their peers, they spent more time in mixed-gender groups than other girls and tended to retaliate more.

Figure 4.5 Can you explain this boy's behaviour by using material from each of the four explanations in this chapter, and by referring to the information on gender and cultural differences?

The consistent pattern of gender differences in levels of aggression, regardless of the cultural setting, suggests that innate factors such as genes and hormones play a major part in aggression (see Biological factors in sex differences, p.158). Nevertheless, social learning theory explains how these innate differences become established, because the child imitates models who are similar, so boys imitate males, girls imitate females, children who are aggressive will imitate aggressive models.

 ## Cultural differences

If **cross-cultural** evidence shows similar patterns of aggressive behaviour in many cultures, this suggests that it is largely determined by biological forces: it is due to nature. If there are variations between cultures, this suggests that nurture (the environment and experience) has a key role in aggressive behaviour. Let us review some of the evidence that levels of aggression vary in different cultures:

● Societies differ in their tolerance of aggression. In some cultures, violence is a key feature because of conflict between groups, for example, in Israel, Palestine, or Iraq.

- Sub-cultures within a society may differ in their attitudes. Religious groups such as the Amish or the Quakers stress non-violence, whereas terrorist or criminal groups may use violence to achieve their aims.
- Bronfenbrenner (1970) compared the way children were reared in the USA and in Russia. He found that co-operation and a sense of community spirit were predominant in Russian culture at that time, whereas the American children, who were encouraged to be independent, saw aggression in the media and in sports settings, even though it was not necessarily encouraged in the home.
- The cultural context determines which acts are to be considered aggressive. One study described a tribe in New Guinea which practised head-hunting. However, it was part of a religious ritual and therefore not considered aggressive. It is these kinds of differences which make comparisons between cultures so complex.
- Some research has found that there is a consistent level of aggression across various activities within the same culture. E. Ebbeson and colleagues (1975) compared the hostility of countries (in their relationships with neighbouring countries) and type of games played. They found that the more warlike the culture, the more aggressive the games.

The research suggests that because there are wide variations in levels of aggression shown in different cultural groups, there is a learned element to aggression. However, whether members of an aggressive culture learn to show aggression, or on the other hand members of a non-aggressive culture learn to repress or re-direct innate aggression, is still not clear.

Finally, conflict between cultures may be explained by H. Tajfel and J. Turner's (1986) social identity theory (see Attitudes of prejudice, p.103). They propose that we gain self-esteem from the group to which we belong, so we tend to exaggerate the positive aspects of our own group. In addition, in order to feel better about our own group, we denigrate other groups. This is a basis for prejudice, discrimination and possibly aggression between cultures.

The OCR exam

The OCR exam will test your ability to:
- demonstrate an understanding of the basic principles of social learning theory
- describe the social learning theory explanation of human aggression
- consider gender and cultural differences in the level of aggression and the possible role of the media
- evaluate the social learning theory of aggression in terms of non-behavioural explanations, e.g. Freud.

Sample exam questions on aggression

1. From your study of psychology describe the Social Learning theory of aggression. (5 marks)

2. a What was the research method used in Bandura's study? (1 mark)

   b Explain one advantage and one disadvantage of this method. (2+2 marks)

3. Describe what is meant by correlation in psychological research. (2 marks)

4. Identify two possible factors other than television which might produce aggressive behaviour. (2 marks)

5. Describe one non-behavioural explanation of aggression, e.g. Freud. (6 marks)

6. Describe one cultural difference in the level of aggression. (2 marks)

Developmental Psychology

Developmental psychology is concerned with the ways in which people change over their life span. This is illustrated in the next two chapters.

Chapter 5 concerns Attachment, how it develops and what might happen when attachments go wrong. Chapter 6 looks at Cognitive Development, particularly Piaget's theory about how children's thinking develops.

Attachment

The newborn infant is utterly dependent on others if it is to survive – others provide food, warmth and protection. This helplessness seems to act like a magnet, attracting the adult's attention and care. Psychologists have studied how the relationship between the baby and its carers develops, and its importance for the child's long-term development. We will look at some of the research in this chapter as we consider the role of mothers as main carers. Finally we survey the variety of ways that children are cared for in different cultures.

The development of attachments

An attachment can be defined as:

● a close emotional relationship with another person.

Infant behaviours such as crying, making eye contact, reaching and grasping form the basis of the baby's interaction with others. These behaviours invite carers to respond to the baby, to attract its attention, make it smile or to understand its needs. This is how attachments form, from the interaction between the two people.

For the first three months, most babies respond equally to any care-giver, but then they start to respond more to the people who are familiar to them. So a baby may wave its arms or smile when it sees its father's face, but there will be little reaction from the baby when it sees a stranger. The baby continues to respond most to those it interacts with frequently until about six or seven months of age. It then begins to show a special preference – an **attachment** – to certain people. We consider that the baby has formed an attachment to someone when it shows two particular behaviours:

- **separation distress** – for example, if the baby cries when its mother leaves the room, we conclude that the baby feels insecure when the mother is out of sight
- **stranger fear** – if a stranger comes close to the baby and it moves away from the stranger and towards another person, we conclude that it is fearful of strangers and gains security from this person.

Some babies show these behaviours much more frequently and intensely than others, but nevertheless they are seen as evidence that the baby has formed an **attachment** when it looks to that person for security, comfort and protection. Such an attachment has usually developed by one year old.

Figure 5.1 This baby may be showing stranger fear

The security of attachments

By the security of the child's attachment we mean how confident the child is that its special person will provide what it needs. The security of a one-year-old's attachment to its mother was tested by M. Ainsworth (1978) in her 'Strange Situation' studies. These were **controlled observations** in which observers noted children's behaviour when mothers and strangers came into and left the room. Ainsworth concluded that the type of attachment children showed could be classed as secure or insecure – but there were two types of insecurity. Details of the percentage of children showing the three attachment types are shown in Table 5.1.

Type of attachment	% of children	Attachment behaviours
Securely attached	70	Happy when mother present, distressed by her absence, went to her quickly when she returned, a stranger provided little comfort
Insecurely attached – anxious-avoidant	15	Avoided the mother, indifferent to her presence or absence, greatest distress when child alone, a stranger could comfort just as well as the mother
Insecurely attached – anxious-resistant	15	Seemed unsure of mother, more anxious about mother's presence, distress in her absence, would go to her quickly when she returned then struggle to get away, also resisted strangers

Table 5.1 Ainsworth's three types of attachment

Evaluation of Ainsworth's research

The Strange Situation has been used by other researchers who have found it a useful way of identifying attachment types. These three types have been found consistently, though M. Main and J. Soloman (1985) identified a third type of insecure attachment, which they called **disorganised attachment**, in which children seemed dazed or confused and showed avoidance and clinging at the same time.

However, Ainsworth has been criticised for classifying children's attachment style solely on the basis of the child's response to its mother. The child may have a different type of attachment to the father or grandmother, for example. In addition, some research has shown that the same child may show different types of attachment on two different occasions. It appears that this may be due to changes in the child's circumstances, so for example a securely attached child may appear insecurely attached if the mother becomes ill or the family circumstances change.

Methodological criticisms focus on the artificial nature of the **laboratory experiment**. It seems that children show much stronger attachment behaviours in the laboratory setting (a strange situation) than they do at home, which suggests that the design of this research actually distorts the subject it is studying – attachment behaviour. Ainsworth also contravened ethical guidelines by causing **distress** to the children, although the mother's **consent** was gained and if she wished to **withdraw** her child at any point she could do so.

Good attachments seem to be related to other aspects of the child's development. Securely attached children also tend to show the following:

- the ability to get along with others
- good emotional development, showing confidence, trust in others and self-esteem
- flexibility and resourcefulness
- longer attention span, more confidence in attempting problems and they use their mothers more effectively for assistance.

These findings show a **correlation**, but one of the psychologists who felt that a secure attachment was the *cause* of good long-term development was John Bowlby, whose work we now turn to.

Bowlby's theory of attachment

John Bowlby was working from the 1940s until the 1980s. He was a psychoanalyst, believing that early experiences have a profound effect on later life, and his ideas on attachment have been controversial. Bowlby's theory of attachment (1969) proposed that attachment is innate in both infant and the main care-giver, usually the mother, and that the formation of this attachment is crucial for the infant's survival and development. The key aspects of his theory are described below.

- **Innate** – the infant is biologically programmed to cry, cling, make eye contact, smile and recognise human faces and sounds. Equally, the mother (or substitute mother) is programmed to respond to these behaviours. As they do so, this mutual attachment develops and both infant and mother feel anxiety when separated.
- **Monotropy** – by 6–8 months of age the child shows separation anxiety and stranger fear (as we saw in Ainsworth's research), which demonstrates its attachment to the mother. Bowlby claimed that this was its main attachment and was different from all others, so the father had no special emotional importance for the child.
- **Development** – the mother provides security and a safe base from which the child can explore its world, thus promoting its cognitive development (see Chapter 5). This unique relationship builds trust, so it provides expectations about others which in turn affect all the child's future relationships. Attachment is as essential for the child's psychological wellbeing as food is for its physical wellbeing, claims Bowlby.
- **Critical period** – Bowlby's views were influenced by attachment behaviours in young animals, for example, newly-hatched ducklings follow the mother closely wherever she goes. He proposed that the human infant was genetically programmed to form an attachment, and that there was a **critical period** between about six months and three years of age during which the baby can most easily

form an attachment. Because the critical period is biologically programmed, Bowlby argued that if an attachment has not formed during this time, it will probably be too late.

Bowlby's stress on the importance of this attachment is underlined by his prediction that if it failed to develop, or was damaged in the first five years of life, there would be long-term and irreversible problems in the child's emotional, social and cognitive development. He called this maternal deprivation and we look at this in more detail later in the chapter, on p.65.

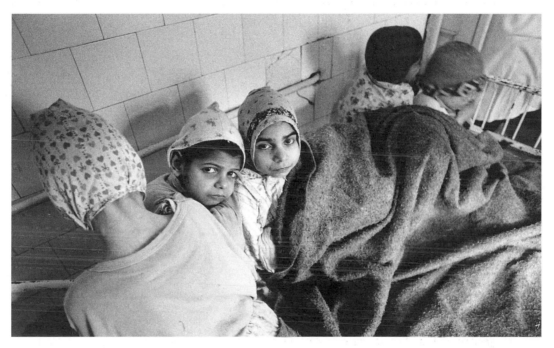

Figure 5.2 Bowlby would say these orphans are likely to have suffered permanent damage because they have experienced maternal deprivation

An evaluation of Bowlby's theory of attachment

Bowlby's theory offered a comprehensive explanation for the development of attachments and stressed the importance of attachments for the child's long-term development. His evidence was crucial in changing childcare practices in, for example, hospitals. Emphasis shifted towards the emotional needs of the child, parents were encouraged to be with the child in hospital: nursing care and the ward itself became child-centred. His ideas helped form attitudes about women in the 1950s – that their proper roles should be as mothers and homemakers (see Gender role, p.158).

Bowlby's theory generated much research, some of which disproved or modified it. For example, children with a poor attachment to their mother do not always have poor relationships with others, whether adults or peers. Critics also argue that the reason for good relationships with mother and others, or of poor relationships with mother and others, could depend on how good children are at forming relationships with anyone.

Below we look at research which criticises Bowlby's claim for a critical period and for monotropy, the special nature of the mother–child relationship.

Is there a critical period?

If children who are not able to form an attachment with their mothers are able to form attachments later in life, after the age of three, this refutes Bowlby's claim for a critical period for the development of an attachment.

Evidence that main attachments can form later comes from a **longitudinal study** by B. Tizard, J. Rees and J. Hodges (1978). They followed the development of children who had been in institutionalised care (residential nurseries) from only a few months of age until they were three years old. Some were then adopted, some returned to their mothers, some remained in the nursery. There was also a **control group**: these children had spent all their lives with their own families.

When assessed at eight years old, the institutionalised children who had been adopted had developed good attachments. Their social and intellectual development was better than that of children who had left the nursery to return to their own families. This suggests that there is not a critical period for the development of attachments, and also that the best place for children is not always with their own mothers, which is what Bowlby claimed.

Is there a special mother–child relationship?

There are several aspects of this claim which have been criticised; the research by R. Schaffer and P. Emerson (1964) is an example. They used **naturalistic observation** and **interviews** over 12 months to discover more about how infants develop attachments during their first year or so of life. Schaffer and Emerson's results contradict Bowlby because they found that:

- The mother was the main attachment figure for about half of the children at 18 months old; for the rest the father was the main figure.
- Many of the babies had more than one attachment by ten months old; attachment figures included mother, father, grandparents, brothers, sisters and neighbours.
- Attachments were most likely to form with those who responded accurately to the baby's signals, which Schaffer and Emerson called 'sensitive responsiveness'. If the

main carer ignored the baby's signals then there was often greater attachment to someone the baby saw less, but who responded to it more sensitively.

 M. Rutter (1982) evaluated Bowlby's ideas using a wide range of evidence and concluded that the quality of the child's main attachments are actually very similar, although one may be stronger than the rest. So children seem to form several attachments at quite a young age, and these are based on the way each person interacts with the child. This suggests that the child's attachment to the mother is based on the quality of the mother's care, rather than any biological factors.

Findings from studies such as these contradict Bowlby's claim that the attachment to the mother is different in quality to any other attachments. Indeed we have seen that the main attachment may be to the father, who Bowlby claimed was much less important for the child emotionally.

Figure 5.3 Who explains this father's relationship with his son better – Bowlby or Schaffer and Emerson? Why?

The long-term effects of privation and deprivation

Bowlby's prediction about the long-term effects of a damaged attachment, or no attachment at all (which is called his **maternal deprivation** hypothesis) was based on his work with emotionally disturbed juveniles (young people) during the 1940s.

He investigated their early years using the **case study** method. This involved **interviews**, and looking at past school and medical records. Bowlby divided the young people into two groups with 44 participants in each. One group comprised juvenile thieves, the other consisted of juveniles who were emotionally disturbed but had no known criminal involvement. His results showed that:

- More than half of the juvenile thieves had been separated from their mothers for longer than six months during their first five years, but in the other group only two had such a separation.
- Several of the young thieves showed affectionless psychopathy (they were not able to care about or feel affection for others).

Bowlby concluded that the reason for the anti-social behaviour in the juvenile thieves was due to separation from their mothers.

This special attachment to the mother represents an internal working model for the child's relationships with others, proposed Bowlby, so if the child has a secure attachment it is able to form good relationships in later life. If maternal deprivation occurred this could jeopardise the development of future relationships. Even a bad home was preferable to a good institution, argued Bowlby, because the child's attachment to the mother can remain intact.

Evaluation of Bowlby's maternal deprivation hypothesis

Once again Bowlby's ideas had a huge impact on society and on research. By identifying a crucial role for mothers in preventing anti-social behaviour, he strengthened moves to encourage women to leave the workplace and stay at home to be mothers. This crucial role for mothers was challenged comprehensively by Michael Rutter, whose work we turn to shortly.

Before doing so, however, we must identify two important methodological criticisms of Bowlby's 'juvenile thieves' study, namely:

- **Weaknesses in the case study method** – this involves retrospective research which is not always reliable because records may be incomplete and people's memory of the past is often biased and partial (see p.175 for details).
- **Correlation** – Bowlby's research only found a relationship between early separation and anti-social behaviour, so he was wrong to conclude that early and long separation from the mother *caused* thieving and affectionless psychopathy. This point is discussed in more detail under Deprivation on p.68.

In a reassessment of Bowlby's ideas, M. Rutter (1982) put forward the view that Bowlby's emphasis on the importance of attachment behaviour and bonding was correct, but he was wrong to identify the mother as the crucial factor. In particular, Rutter asserts that:

- The damaging influences Bowlby cited were due to a variety of circumstances which have different effects, not simply to 'maternal deprivation'.
- The term 'maternal deprivation' masks two very different attachment circumstances: privation and deprivation.

We will look at these points in more detail as we consider privation and deprivation and how they affect children.

Privation

Privation occurs when there is a failure to form an **attachment** to any individual. This may be because the child has a series of different carers or perhaps family discord prevents the development of attachment to any figure. Children experiencing privation do not show distress when separated from a familiar figure, which indicates a lack of attachment. Many of the juvenile thieves Bowlby studied had had several homes and many carers, suggesting that they could have failed to form any attachments – they were **privated**.

Research indicates that such privation may indeed be related to anti-social behaviour, affectionless psychopathy, and disorders of language, intellectual development and physical growth. However, these problems are not due solely to the lack of attachment to a mother figure, as Bowlby claimed, but to factors such as the lack of intellectual stimulation and social experiences which attachments normally provide. In contrast to Bowlby's claim, such problems can be overcome later in the child's development, with the right kind of care.

Evidence for this comes from Tizard, Rees and Hodges's study (see p.64) as well as research on children in an orphanage conducted by H. Skeels and colleagues (1949). They monitored a group of one- and two-year-olds as they were moved to a home for mentally retarded girls. Their **mean** IQ was 64, but after two years in the home this had increased to 92 (100 is the norm of intelligence for the general population). The children who remained in the orphanage had a **mean** IQ of 86, but two years later this had dropped to 60.

None of the children had a mother or permanent mother substitute, yet one group thrived whilst the other did not. Skeels concluded this was because the children in the home had plenty of attention and stimulation from the girls, whereas those in the orphanage had much less. This suggests that it is not the lack of a mother which may cause developmental problems, but the lack of stimulation and affection, so the effects of **privation** can be overcome with the right kind of care.

Finally, there have been a few case studies of children who have experienced extreme privation, being locked up by their carers, often deprived of food, light and exercise as well as the company of other humans. Even in these cases, if the child is given plenty of love, care and stimulation it seems to be able to recover without extensive long-term damage. However, if this quality of care is not available, or if the child has reached adolescence, then long-term damage is evident.

Deprivation

Deprivation occurs when the child has developed an attachment but is then separated from the attachment figure. M. Rutter (1976) argued that Bowlby had only found that maternal deprivation was related to long-term problems, not that deprivation was the cause. He studied 2,000 boys living on the Isle of Wight and in London, focusing on the relationship between separation and delinquency.

The results showed that when separation was due to the mother's illness or death, there was no correlation with delinquency. However, when separation was due to discord in the family home, or to the mother's mental illness, boys were much more likely to become delinquent. Rutter concluded that the long-term effects of **deprivation** showed:

● An increase in anti-social behaviour where the separation had been related to family discord or a history of disturbance in the life of the young person. There appeared to be few ill-effects when separations were due to holidays, hospitalisation or when the child had experienced successful separations previously. In this last case the child may have established a secure attachment which enabled it to withstand separations.
● A change in the nature of the child's attachment: it may become more insecure. The child may show separation anxiety for a year or longer. However, children with a secure attachment seem to be able to withstand the effects of deprivation more than children whose attachment is insecure.
● Children differ in their ability to cope with the effects of deprivation; factors such as the age of the child, its temperament and gender affect the ability to cope with the disruption of their attachments.

GROUP ACTIVITY – Alternative explanations

Look again at Figure 5.2. Bowlby would say these orphans may show long-term permanent damage because they have experienced maternal deprivation. From what you have read in this chapter, how would you answer the following questions:

1 What experiences (apart from maternal deprivation) might these orphans have had?
2 Do you think Bowlby is right – that damage is permanent? Break into two groups and discuss this question. One group must present a case supporting Bowlby, the other group's case must argue against Bowlby. Whose argument is the more powerful? Why?

Psychologists such as Ann and Alan Clarke (1976) argue that children are much more resilient than Bowlby believed, that the early years are simply the first stage in life, and that subsequent experiences also have considerable influence on the child's development. As we have seen above, if later experiences are positive then the outcome in the long term is likely to be good. But where a poor start is followed by more damaging experiences the outcome may also be poor.

Cultural variations in childcare practices

Research of childcare practices in various cultures helps us to see patterns in behaviour, whether there may be a link between particular types of practice and long-term effects, to compare the role of the mother as well as the effects of different child-rearing practices. For example, Ainsworth (1967) studied babies in Uganda aged from four months old to two years old, **observing** them every fortnight for nine months and **interviewing** the mothers. She classified the babies as securely attached, insecurely attached and not yet attached, finding that the higher the mother's sensitivity and holding of the baby, the more secure the attachment was. She also found that most infants were cared for by several adults, so they formed multiple attachments.

Several studies of childcare practices in various cultures have used Ainsworth's Strange Situation: results of studies in Japan, Israel and Germany can be seen in Figure 5.4.

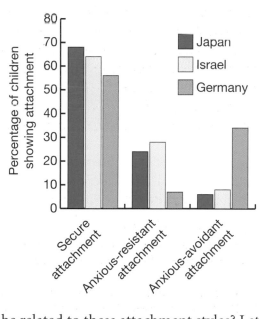

Figure 5.4 Bar chart showing types of attachment in various cultures based on the Strange Situation

How might childcare arrangements be related to these attachment styles? Let us consider this by examining the way children are looked after in each of these countries, based on a cross-cultural comparison of results from the Strange Situation.

In Japan close family relationships are highly valued and children spend very little time apart from their mothers, who are very responsive to their children. Children are also encouraged to develop a group identity and co-operate with others. The relatively high level of **anxious-resistant** attachments may be explained by the intense distress of children who were rarely left with anyone else. They also showed low levels of **anxious-avoidant** attachments, which may be explained by the constant and responsive care given by the mother.

The Israeli children who were studied lived on a kibbutz, living in a children's house rather than with their parents. They were cared for and educated by a number of people in the nursery, spending only a small amount of time with their parents in the early evening. They also developed close relationships with the other children in their house. We can see from Fig. 5.4 that Israeli children showed similar attachment patterns to the Japanese, though they had completely different relationships with their mothers. Again, the presence of a stranger for children who have always been surrounded by familiar faces may account for the high percentage of **anxious-resistant** and low proportion of **anxious-avoidant** attachments.

German mothers, although caring and responsive, encouraged their children to be independent and not to be demanding or clinging. They tended to keep a distance between themselves and the child. Here there was a lower percentage of **secure** attachments than that found in other countries, but a higher level of **anxious-avoidant** attachments, where the child pays little attention to the caregiver, whether she leaves or returns. It appears that this style of childcare is related to more independent and non-clinging children.

Evaluation of cross-cultural research in childcare practices

Although it is useful to examine how childcare practices may be related to attachment styles, the results from cross-cultural studies may not be very reliable. Here are some reasons why:

- As these are not **experimental studies**, we cannot be sure that childcare practices cause particular attachment styles.
- The basis of the Strange Situation study is that a child who shows separation anxiety has a secure attachment, but the excessive distress of the Japanese child may reflect the unusual nature of the situation for them, rather than reflect the quality of their attachment.
- The researchers' interpretation of behaviour in another culture may be biased, unless the researchers are from the same culture as that which they are studying.
- There may be as much variation in childcare within a culture as between two cultures. This is a point made by M. van Ijzendoorn and P. Kroonenberg (1988), who noted that two studies in Japan showed different patterns. One found the

percentage of different types to be similar to Ainsworth's, but the other found no **anxious-avoidant** and a considerable number of **anxious-resistant** styles of attachment.

Despite variations between cultures, J. Kagan and colleagues (1978) report that there is remarkable consistency in the appearance of **separation distress** at about seven months of age, suggesting an innate basis for the development of attachment.

The OCR exam

The OCR exam will test your ability to:

- be aware of the development of early human attachment, e.g. fearful reactions, secure and insecure attachments
- describe and evaluate Bowlby's theory of attachment
- consider the possible long-term effects of deprivation and privation
- demonstrate knowledge of some cultural variations in child-care practices.

Sample exam questions on attachment

1. From Figure 5.4, in which country were the highest level of anxious-avoidant children? (1 mark)
2. Describe the main characteristics of Ainsworth's secure attachment. (2 marks)
3. Describe Bowlby's theory of attachment. (4 marks)
4. Explain one criticism of Bowlby's theory of attachment. (3 marks)
5. Identify and describe two types of observation. (2+2 marks)
6. Explain the difference between privation and deprivation in attachment theory. (4 marks)
7. Describe real-life examples of situations where infants may experience:
   a separation (2 marks)
   b reunion. (2 marks)
8. Explain cultural variations in childcare practices. (6 marks)

Cognitive Development

Imagine that your teacher showed you two pieces of string side by side, of the same length, and then scrunched one up. You would know it was still the same length as the other one; but a four-year-old child would not. This shows that our understanding of the world changes as we grow up, that we think about things in a different way. This chapter looks at the work of Jean Piaget, who developed a theory of how thinking, or cognition, develops from infancy to adulthood.

Piaget's theory of cognitive development

In Jean Piaget's early work with children he asked them questions, and was interested to discover that when children gave the wrong answers they were often the same kind of wrong answers. After further research he proposed that the way children think is different from adults, and that it develops in stages from infancy to adulthood. Piaget argued that these changes in thinking are biologically based. This means that every child goes through these same stages in the development of their thinking (or cognition) as they mature to adulthood.

As Piaget worked with children he came to the conclusion that children were actively trying to make sense of the world – he called them little scientists because of the way they explore and test it. They do this using whatever skills they have. For example, a baby uses its ability to grasp in order to hold on to something. But the baby who tries to hold a bottle must change the shape of its hands and be able to make them work together. Piaget proposed that this development in thinking required two processes which he called **assimilation** and **accommodation**.

The infant's grasping ability is inborn (or innate) and the baby has been using this skill for some weeks to grasp fingers or clothes. This is **assimilation**, which means using a skill in several, very similar ways. However, as the 'little scientist' explores its world it will come across a situation in which its present skills are inadequate. In order to hold the bottle the baby must adapt its grasping skill: this process of adaptation is called **accommodation**. Once it has succeeded in holding the bottle it will use this new holding skill again and again in many situations – assimilation.

Piaget identified four stages of cognitive development, and you will see shortly that children's thinking changes in each of these stages: these changes develop through the processes of assimilation and accommodation. Now we will look at each of the stages, focusing on research which demonstrates what the child can, or cannot, do.

Sensorimotor stage (birth–two years)

The baby explores its world using its senses (sight, sound, taste, touch and so on) in combination with body movements. Initially these movements are reflexes, such as the grasping or sucking reflex, and they form the basis for its exploration. For example, the infant watches a moving object, reaches out towards it and after many attempts is able to grasp the object. A few weeks later the baby will then be able to bring the object to its mouth, and explore it using its sense of taste and smell. Gradually these skills develop and become more complex.

Figure 6.1 This baby is using its sensorimotor skills to understand its world

Object permanence

One major characteristic of this stage is the development of **object permanence**. To begin with, the baby lacks object permanence, it acts as though objects no longer exist if they are not seen. When Piaget shook a toy in front of a four-month-old it reached out for it. When a cover was placed over the toy, the baby looked away and appeared to lose interest, as though the the toy had never existed. However, when Piaget repeated the actions in front of an eight-month-old, the baby continued to reach for the toy, sometimes showing distress at its disappearance.

From this behaviour Piaget inferred that by eight months old the child has developed an internal representation of the object – the child can retain an image of it – which is why it continues to reach for it and show distress that it has disappeared. The baby has therefore achieved object permanence.

Pre-operational stage (two–seven years)

By two years of age the toddler starts to use symbols, signs or objects to represent things. This is an example of **symbolic thinking**, which is when we make something 'stand for' something else. For example, the three-year-old will use a cardboard box as a house or a car. Language is evidence of symbolic thinking, because the child knows that when you say 'table' the word 'stands for' an actual table – he could draw one or point one out in the room or tell you how you could use a table. Piaget said that language skills develop as a result of the child's cognitive development.

Another feature of the pre-operational stage is **animism**. Children up to about four years old think that inanimate objects have feelings like they do (this is animism), saying, for example, 'The flowers are tired' when flowers are wilting. A possible explanation for animism is described in the next characteristic, egocentrism.

Egocentrism

Have you ever played hide and seek with a three-year-old who hides by standing in front of you covering her eyes? Because she cannot see *you* she thinks you cannot see *her*; this is an example of egocentric thinking (or **egocentrism**), a characteristic of the pre-operational stage. Piaget argued that the child understands the world only from its own viewpoint, thinking others have the same views and experiences as it does.

J. Piaget and B. Inhelder (1956) devised the 'three mountains' task to test children's egocentric thinking (see Figure 6.2). The child sat at a large, table-top model of three mountains and was asked what he could see from his side of the table. A doll was then placed at various positions around the table. The child was shown photographs of the mountains taken from these different positions, and asked to indicate which of them showed the doll's view.

Figure 6.2 A child doing the 'three mountains' task

Four- and five-year-old children thought the doll's view would be the same as their own, which indicates **egocentrism**. However, most seven-year-olds identified the doll's view correctly, which suggests that their thinking is no longer egocentric. One of the causes of egocentrism may be that the child tends to take notice of only *one* feature of a situation, so he is unable to notice or understand two different features of a situation. This may be because he cannot represent both features to himself at the same time, so this leads to errors in his understanding. **Centration** was the term Piaget used for this focus on only one feature.

Concrete operational stage (seven–eleven years)

Early in the concrete operational stage the child starts to be able to **de-centre**, to take account of two contradictory features of a situation. This is why the child's thinking is no longer egocentric in the 'three mountains' task. Another example of de-centring is **conservation**, the ability to understand that something is the same, even though its appearance changes. Take the example of the piece of string at the start of this chapter: your knowledge that the length is the same, even though it is scrunched up, shows that you can **conserve** length.

Conservation

Piaget and his colleagues showed a child two identical glasses, each filled with liquid to the same level. When asked if one glass contained more than the other, or if they both contained the same amount, the child said they were the same. Then the liquid was poured from one glass into a taller but narrower glass. When the question was repeated, a four-year-old child would usually say the taller glass had more. Because the level of the liquid has changed, the child thinks the amount has changed, usually saying there is more in the taller glass because it is higher. Their understanding is dominated by what they see, by appearances. In other words, they centrate on what they see, according to Piaget.

However, seven-year-olds would tell you the amount was the same – this indicates that they are able to conserve because they are not deceived by appearances. They can remember the initial state of the liquid *and* the process by which its appearance was changed (we say they show conservation of liquid). This ability to take into account two features of the situation shows that they can **de-centre**.

The child's ability to conserve number appears about a year later. Piaget tested this by setting out a row of six sweets and asking the child to make another row the same as the first one (as shown in Figure 6.3). Piaget then spread out his row of sweets, and asked the child if there was still the same number. If the child knew there was the same number of sweets, this showed they were able to **conserve** number.

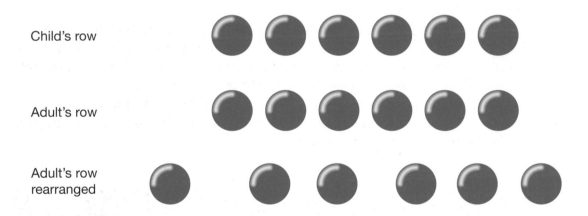

Figure 6.3 The layout of sweets in a conservation of number experiment

Conservation develops slowly but in the same order, with conservation of liquid appearing by about seven years of age, then conservation of length (the scrunched-up string), of number, of weight, with finally conservation of volume appearing at about 11 years old.

When asked why the amount of liquid is the same, the child might answer that if you poured it back into the original glass, it would be the same level; this shows **reversibility** in the child's thinking. This suggests that the child can think in a logical sequence. However, it first needs the opportunity to work through sequences with actual objects (which is why this is called the *concrete* operations stage).

Formal operational stage (eleven years and older)

The child in the previous stage could manipulate things, but in the formal operational stage the child can manipulate ideas. A simple example is the ability to envisage relationships, as in the following problem:

> If Mark is taller than Ali, and Mark is smaller than Kerry, who is the tallest?

In the previous stage the child would have to draw a picture or use different-sized objects to solve this problem. Now the child can manipulate the ideas in its head. It can do mathematical calculations, think creatively, imagine the outcome of particular actions.

The child is also able to solve problems in a systematic way, as is demonstrated in one of Piaget's tests for the formal operational stage. B. Inhelder and J. Piaget (1958) gave a child five containers of colourless liquids (chemicals), one of which was called the 'indicator'. The task was to find which combination of chemicals turned the 'indicator' yellow. The formal operational child will test the liquids systematically, changing only one thing at a time. In other words, the child acts like a scientist, controlling all variables except one (see Independent variable and dependent variable, p.178).

The child may also continue to test *all* combinations, even though one has already turned the 'indicator' yellow. Children who have not achieved the formal operational stage try combinations in a haphazard way rather than systematically, and usually stop as soon as they find a combination that works.

According to Piaget, once the young person has achieved formal operational thinking, there is no further change in structure of thinking, only in the complexity, flexibility and level of abstraction.

An evaluation of Piaget's research methodology

Piaget used three research methods, each of which has strengths and weaknesses. They are covered in more detail in Chapter 13. Here we will consider how Piaget used them:

- **Naturalistic observation** – these observations were mainly of his own children and he was the only observer. The tendency for observers to be biased or to interpret behaviour in a particular way can be counteracted by using two or more observers, but Piaget did not do this. **Generalisations** should not be made from informal research such as this, but Piaget did generalise and many of the ideas in his sensorimotor and pre-operational stages are based on these observations.
- **Clinical interviews** – Piaget asked children questions, and tailored the questions to each child as he talked to them. If they did not understand the question

he tried to make it clearer, if they gave an interesting answer he pursued it. He wanted to follow the way the child thought, without distorting or stopping it. Although this enabled him to tease out patterns in children's thinking, he came to feel that the clinical interview depended too much on what the children actually said; he was concerned that the children knew more than they could actually explain and that their answers were 'shaped' by his questions.

● **Experiments** – he began to use formal experiments more, manipulating variables and treating all the children in much the same way, with standard tasks and instructions. Nevertheless, his **sample** sizes were fairly small, and although more rigorous, the designs of these experiments have been criticised for producing biased results. Psychologists have modified these experiments in order to eliminate the design weaknesses, and some of these critical research studies are described below.

Critical research studies

A challenge for anyone who studies young children is finding a way of assessing just what the child understands. Children may understand a concept, but the researcher has to find a way of enabling them to demonstrate that understanding. Research on babies is restricted because they cannot use language, so their understanding must be inferred from their behaviour.

Language skills in children of under seven are limited, and this affects their ability to follow instructions, understand questions and express themselves accurately. Piaget himself argued that the development of language depends on cognitive development, so a child who understands a particular concept may still not have developed the language skills to talk about it.

A further criticism of Piaget's research is that he underestimated the social influences which affect children's understanding and behaviour. Children use other people to help them make sense of things, they think adults are more knowledgeable, they like to please strangers. You will see below how some of these factors may have influenced Piaget's findings, according to research which has investigated several of the abilities described above.

Object permanence

Research on object permanence has shown that children do *not* lose interest when they can no longer see an object. In T. Bower and J. Wishart's (1972) experiment babies less than four months old were filmed in a laboratory using an infra-red camera. A toy was offered to the baby, but as it reached for the toy, the light in the laboratory was switched off. The infra-red camera showed that the baby continued to reach for the toy, even though it was no longer visible.

This suggests that objects do still exist in the baby's mind, even though they are not visible. One explanation for Piaget's findings is that the baby is distracted by the movement of the cover as it is placed over the toy, which is why it looks away and appears to 'forget' having been interested in the toy. The distractibility of the infant may be explained by cognitive factors such as limited attention span or memory, which Piaget did not take into account. By eliminating the distracting movement, Bower and Wishart's research reveals different behaviour, and possibly a difference in the infant's understanding.

Figure 6.4 This child loses interest in the toy directly it is covered up

However, there is evidence for Piaget's claim that once the baby develops a mental representation of an object it understands that it still exists even though it is not seen. Studies of attachment in young children demonstrate that at about eight months of age, babies show **stranger fear** (see p.60). According to the concept of object permanence, they have developed mental representations of the people they are attached to, so when someone appears who does not match any of those representations, the child shows alarm or fear.

Egocentrism

Piaget's 'three mountains' task has been criticised because it did not make sense to the children tested. It was also made more difficult because the child had to match the doll's 'view' with a photograph.

M. Hughes (1975) devised a task which made sense to the child. In a model comprising two intersecting walls, a 'boy' doll and two 'policeman' dolls, the researcher placed a policeman doll in various positions and asked the child to hide the boy doll from the policeman (see Figure 6.5).

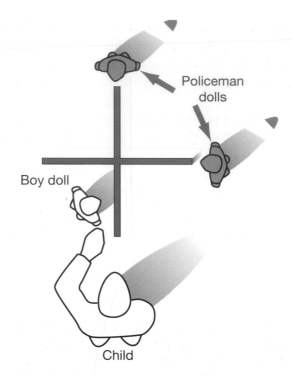

Figure 6.5 The layout of Hughes' experiment on egocentrism

The child needed to take the perspective of the boy doll *and* the policeman doll, and most children between four and five years old were able to hide the boy doll successfully, even when it had to be hidden from *two* policeman dolls. This suggests that children have largely lost their egocentric thinking by five years of age. Hughes's experiment allowed them to demonstrate this because the task made sense to the child, whereas Piaget's did not.

Conservation

Several aspects of the conservation tasks have been criticised: for example, that they fail to take account of the social context of the child's understanding. S. Rose and M. Blank (1974) argued that when a child gives the wrong answer to a question, adults often repeat the question in order to hint that the first answer was wrong. This is what Piaget did by asking children the same question twice, before and after the liquid was poured into another glass. By doing this he suggested that the child's first answer ('They are the same') was wrong, so the child changed its answer.

When Rose and Blank replicated this experiment but asked the question *once*, after the liquid had been poured, they found many more six-year-olds gave the correct answer. This shows children can conserve at a younger age than Piaget claimed, and suggests that the design of his experiment prevented them from showing this ability.

Another feature of the conservation task which may interfere with children's understanding is that the adult purposely alters the appearance of something, so the child thinks this alteration is important. J. McGarrigle and M. Donaldson (1974) devised an experiment on conservation of number in which the alteration was accidental.

When the two rows of sweets were laid out and the child was satisfied there were the same number, a 'naughty teddy' appeared and whilst playing around, actually messed up one row of sweets. Once he was safely back in a box the children were asked if there was the same number of sweets. The children were between four and six years old, and more than half gave the correct answer. This suggests that, once again, Piaget's design interfered with the child's understanding of the situation, leading him to underestimate the child's cognitive abilities.

GROUP ACTIVITY – Writing up a procedure

Imagine that you are going to replicate Rose and Blank's experiment. With a partner, plan your procedure carefully and write it up. Use the information on Procedure (see p.193) as a guide. Remember that someone else should be able to repeat what you did by following this description.

When the write-up is finished, each pair in the group must read out their Procedure to the others in the group. Still working in pairs, evaluate each write-up as it is presented and award marks out of 5.

A summary evaluation of Piaget's theory

Below is a list of criticisms, some of which have been discussed above. Finally, a summary of the value of Piaget's work is presented.

- The changes in intellectual development which Piaget identified occur at a younger age than he claimed.
- He failed to take sufficient account of the child's social environment.
- His methods were not rigorous enough.
- Some of his concepts are rather vague, and development seems to be more continuous than the stages he identified.
- Piaget provides more of a description of cognitive development than an explanation for it.

Piaget's theory has had a major influence on our understanding of cognitive development and has provided a framework for research. Aspects of it have been challenged and alternative explanations have been offered, but the abilities he identified, and the sequence of their appearance, remain intact. His ideas have been widely accepted and used to enrich children's cognitive development in school and pre-school settings.

The OCR exam

The OCR exam will test your ability to:

- demonstrate knowledge and understanding of Piaget's stage theory of cognitive development
- describe some of Piaget's research and findings, e.g. object permanence, egocentrism, conservation
- evaluate Piaget's research methodology
- evaluate Piaget's theory in the light of critical research studies, e.g. McGarrigle and Donaldson.

Sample exam questions on cognitive development

1. Name the first of Piaget's stages of cognitive development. (1 mark)
2. Describe the main characteristics of the concrete operational stage. (2 marks)
3. Describe what is meant by 'egocentrism' in Piaget's theory. (2 marks)
4. What was the aim of the study by Bower and Wishart (p.78)? (1 mark)
5. Several studies have been carried out which are critical of Piaget's theory.
   a Outline how one of these studies was carried out. (3 marks)
   b Outline the findings from this study. (3 marks)
6. Outline one criticism of Piaget's research methodology. (2 marks)
7. Identify two ethical issues in psychological research using infants and children. (2+2 marks)

Individual Differentiation

Individual differentiation is concerned with ways that individuals might differ from each other. This is illustrated in the next two chapters.

Chapter 7 considers Aspects of Morality by looking at several explanations for moral development. Chapter 8 explores Attitudes of Prejudice by looking at various types of prejudice and some possible causes.

Aspects of Morality

Morality relates to what is right or wrong, fair or unfair, good or bad. Consider someone who cheats in an exam: we would say it was wrong – it was immoral behaviour. If I asked you *why* it was wrong, then you would be giving your moral reasoning. How does this sense of right and wrong develop? How does it relate to moral behaviour? We will start by looking at three different theories, each of which attempts to answer this question, before we move on to consider possible bias in research into moral development.

Piaget's theory of moral development

Jean Piaget proposed that children's moral development is based on their cognitive development, so both follow the same pattern. His theory of cognitive development is detailed in Chapter 6. Piaget's theory of moral development is based on what the child *says*, which he takes as evidence of the child's understanding and thinking about moral behaviour.

Piaget's research on moral reasoning

Piaget used several techniques to discover the basis of children's moral judgements. He tried to find out how children understand rules using the **clinical interview**. He played marbles with children whilst asking questions about the rules they created, and what would happen if they were broken or did not work very well.

Another technique was to ask questions about the behaviour of children in stories. For instance, in one story a child breaks a cup whilst stealing some jam, in another the child breaks lots of cups by accident. Piaget then asked the child questions such as 'Which child was the naughtiest? Which child should be punished more? Why?'.

Results showed that children under about eight years of age said the child who broke all the cups was the naughtiest, so he was the child who should be punished more. These children were making moral judgements on the basis of the consequences of actions. By eight years old, children were able to make the correct judgement, and take the *intent* into account as well.

Piaget's two stages of moral reasoning

From this research, Piaget (1932) proposed that up to about three or four years old, children are unable to make moral judgements because they do not understand rules, so they cannot understand breaking rules.

Figure 7.1 This game uses rules

Once the child understands rules its moral development goes through these two stages:

● **Heteronomous morality** (morality imposed from outside). The child sees rules as made by parents, teachers, God, and as being unchangeable. Moral judgements are based on rules – if you do something wrong you will be punished. As the child is at the pre-operational stage, thinking shows **centration** – the child can only attend to one aspect of a situation. In Piaget's stories the child attends to the most vivid aspect – the consequences of the action, so the rightness or wrongness of behaviour is based on the *consequences* of an action. Piaget called this **moral realism**, and children show it up to about eight years old.

- **Autonomous morality** (morality based on your own rules). This appears when the child is able to de-centre, so he can judge the intent behind the action as well as the consequence. Children now understand that rules can be flexible to suit the situation; they make up their own rules: for example, when playing hide and seek, a younger child will be allowed to count to a lower number. The child's thinking shows **moral relativism** because it is more flexible and can take account of other people's perspectives and needs. Piaget argued that because males play in larger groups than females, this opportunity to take account of others' views and to negotiate rules leads to higher levels of moral reasoning in males.

Evaluation of Piaget's theory of moral development

Although children's moral development does seem to follow this general pattern, there have been criticisms of Piaget's points. For example research suggests that:

- **When the intention is emphasised,** even three-year-olds can make the correct judgements. This echoes criticism that Piaget's theory of cognitive development underestimates children's cognitive abilities (see Piaget's theory of cognitive development, p.81).
- **Girls' moral development** may be more advanced than that of boys, according to some research, which contradicts Piaget's claim. This point is explored in more detail later in this chapter on p.93.
- **The stages are too general** and suggest there is no significant change in moral thinking beyond early adolescence, although research shows that there is. This criticism is addressed in the next cognitive-developmental explanation.

Kohlberg's theory of moral development

Lawrence Kohlberg's theory was based on Piaget's, and is thus cognitive, but it identifies more stages in the developmental process and continues into adulthood. Kohlberg was interested in moral reasoning, and to assess people's moral reasoning he told them a story in which there was a conflict between two ideas of what is right – a moral dilemma. One of his best-known moral dilemmas is the story of Heinz.

Heinz's dilemma

Heinz's wife was dying of cancer. Doctors said a new drug might save her. The drug had been discovered by a pharmacist in Heinz's town but he was charging a lot of money for it – ten times what it cost him to make. Heinz couldn't afford to buy the drug, so he asked friends and relatives to lend him money. But still he only had half the money he needed. He told the pharmacist his wife was dying and asked him to sell the drug cheaper, or asked if he could pay the rest of the money later. The pharmacist said no, he had discovered the drug and was going to make money on it. Heinz got desperate, so he broke into the pharmacy and stole some of the drug.

Kohlberg then asked participants several questions, such as:

Should Heinz have stolen the drug?

Would it change anything if Heinz did not love his wife?

What if the person dying was a stranger; would it make any difference?

Kohlberg's stages of moral reasoning

Kohlberg (1976) conducted a **longitudinal** study, asking ten-year-old boys moral-dilemma questions and continuing every three years for 20 years. Having analysed their answers, Kohlberg proposed that there were three levels of moral reasoning, each having two stages.

Level 1 pre-conventional morality

Authority is outside the individual and reasoning is based on the physical consequences of actions:

- **Stage 1** relates to punishment of actions – if it is punished it must have been wrong. People are obeyed who have greater power.
- **Stage 2** reasoning is based on personal gain such as a reward, or help from someone else – 'The pharmacist should have let Heinz pay later, because one day he might need something from Heinz.'

Level 2 conventional morality

Authority is internalised but not questioned, and reasoning is based on the norms of the group to which the person belongs:

- **Stage 3** answers are related to the approval of others, saying that people like you when you do good things and dislike you when you do bad things.
- **Stage 4** reasoning is based on respect for law and order – not the authority of specific people like parents, but a generalised **social norm** of obedience to authority and doing one's duty.

Level 3 post-conventional morality

Individual judgement is based on self-chosen principles and moral reasoning is based on individual rights and justice:

- **Stage 5** reasoning says that although laws are important, to be fair there are times when they must be changed or ignored. For example, in Heinz's dilemma the protection of life is more important than breaking the law against stealing.
- **Stage 6** answers say that people assume personal responsibility for their actions, based on universal ethical and moral principles which are not necessarily laid down by society. Kohlberg considered that few people ever reached this stage.

GROUP ACTIVITY – Making moral judgements

Working alone, decide whether it is acceptable to do each of the following:

1 Steal sweets in a supermarket.
2 Cheat in an exam.
3 Drive a car without insurance.

Give reasons to justify your answer, then compare your answers as a group. Can you relate the reasons given to any of the levels proposed by Kohlberg?

Kohlberg proposed that the individual's reasoning progresses through each stage, and therefore cannot 'go backwards' from Level 2 to Level 1. He did not tie the levels to a specific age, although research has suggested that Level 1 is up to about ten years old, Level 2 is ten years up to adulthood, and very few adults show Level 3 reasoning. He found that generally males achieved higher levels of moral reasoning than females.

Evaluation of Kohlberg's theory of moral development

Kohlberg's theory does provide more detail than Piaget's and reflects changing levels of moral reasoning in adulthood. However, it has been criticised on several points; for example:

- His studies used only male participants, although some recent research has shown similar results with girls' moral thinking. The gender bias in Kohlberg's research is explored in more detail later in this chapter.

- His theory has been criticised because it is **ethnocentric**, which means he viewed morality from the viewpoint of his own, Western, society. Other cultures have different values; some examples are discussed later on p.93.

- The previous point reflects Kohlberg's failure to take account of the social context of morality. Although Piaget felt that morality developed as a result of the individual's adaptation to his or her own society, he too failed to explain how the social context affects moral reasoning.
- Finally, both these theories focus on moral thinking, yet we do not always behave in accordance with our knowledge of what is right or wrong. Why do we behave in moral, or immoral, ways? The next explanation attempts to answer this question.

Social learning theory

Social learning theory proposes that moral development occurs as a result of the child observing and imitating (or copying) the behaviour of others and being rewarded for that behaviour (see p.43).

According to social learning theory, children are more likely to imitate models who are important to them, perhaps because they are similar to the child, powerful or nurturant, or when the model is reinforced. Children therefore learn moral behaviour by:

- **Observing** the behaviour of people such as parents and teachers (who are powerful and nurturant): for example, when they make sure everyone has an equal-size piece of cake, help someone to push a car that won't start, or say why we should help others. People in the media such as pop stars and footballers are also powerful models.
- **Observing** those of the same sex or age, such as peers and same-sex siblings. The child may imitate their moral behaviour, such as lending a pencil to another child or copying an older brother when he tidies up at home if parents are tired.
- **Reinforcement** for imitating the behaviour. If a boy lends his pencil to another child, who offers a sweet in return, the boy's behaviour has been rewarded and he is more likely to offer help in the future.
- **Imitating** a model whose moral behaviour has been reinforced, which is called **vicarious reinforcement** (or indirect reinforcement).
- **Observing** models who are punished for behaviour which is morally wrong will cause the child to experience **vicarious punishment**. This indirect punishment will deter the child from performing the same immoral behaviour.

One strength of social learning theory is that it explains why children may show moral behaviour in one situation and not in another. For example, a girl watches another girl helping her little brother on a climbing frame and hears the girl's mother say 'What a good sister you are'. The watching child may help *her* little brother next time her own mother is present, but may not help him if there is no-one watching because there is no-one to provide reinforcement.

Through these processes of **observation**, **imitation** and **reinforcement**, the child learns new behaviours and when to perform them. These behaviours gradually become internalised, and eventually the child generates appropriate behaviour without it being modelled. Conducting ourselves in accordance with these internalised standards is rewarding, it increases our feelings of competence about ourselves. A. Bandura (1977) used the term 'self-efficacy' for our sense of competence and appropriateness about our behaviour.

Figure 7.2 Footballers such as Alan Shearer are powerful models. The girls in this photo are less likely to imitate Shearer's behaviour than the boys, according to social learning theory. Why?

 ## Evaluation of social learning theory

Although the theory explains why moral behaviour may vary from situation to situation, it does raise some contradictions. For example:

● Behaviour which is consistent is more likely to be imitated, yet adults are often inconsistent in their behaviour, which means that children are not very likely to imitate the behaviour.

- Children are more likely to copy what they see than what they hear, so if a parent says it is wrong to lie yet the child then hears the parent telling a lie, the child will pay more attention to what the parent *does* (lie) rather than what the parent said (it is wrong). This is related to Piaget's point that children take more notice of the action than the intention.
- The child may be unintentionally reinforced for immoral behaviour. An example is the cartoon below, where the mother has unintentionally reinforced the little girl's behaviour.

Figure 7.3 This little girl has done something wrong but is being rewarded with approval

- Social learning theory predicts that children will learn moral behaviour as a direct result of what they experience. But every child has different experiences, as we have seen in the previous three bullet points. Consequently we would not expect a consistent pattern in children's moral development according to social learning theory, yet we have seen from Piaget's and Kohlberg's research that there *is* a pattern.
- Finally, the theory explains the development of moral behaviour but not the development of the reasoning behind the behaviour.

Bias in research into moral development

Some of the research described above has received criticisms about errors in the design of the research which have in turn biased the results and conclusions. We will consider gender, cultural and methodological bias.

Gender bias

C. Gilligan (1982) criticised the male bias of Kohlberg's research, arguing that because he used male participants, the stages he devised reflected the judgements made by males. Kohlberg's classification gives justice a higher value than caring, because men value justice more than caring, argued Gilligan. This is because men see relationships with others as essentially competitive and needing to be regulated.

Gilligan proposed that women value caring and responsibility more because they are socialised into an **ethic of caring**. She investigated the responses which females

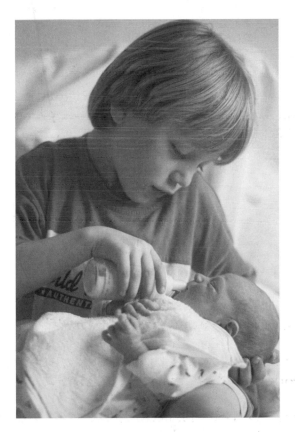

Figure 7.4 According to Gilligan, this boy may be in the minority because girls are more likely to perform caring tasks than boys

gave to real-life dilemmas, and she concluded that women go through three stages of pro-social reasoning:

- **Stage 1** – caring for self.
- **Stage 2** – caring for others.
- **Stage 3** – balancing the requirements of care for self with care for others.

She also concluded that females and males show similar levels of pro-social reasoning, which is supported by other research. However, she *did* find a difference in the emphasis, namely that the pro-social reasoning of females is based on caring rather than justice. Other research has generally failed to find this difference. In fact, the greatest influence on the answers of participants seems to be the kind of dilemmas they are presented with.

In his research on the rules of children's games, Piaget also showed bias towards boys, in that he thought the rules in their games were much more complex than the rules in girls' games. Thus, because of his emphasis on rules, he felt that boys' moral judgements developed more rapidly than those of girls.

Cultural bias

Kohlberg's theory has been criticised because he viewed morality from the viewpoint of his own, Western, society. Being biased towards one's own culture is called **ethnocentrism**. Other cultures have different values which would lead to different types of reasoning and judgements on these moral dilemmas, whereas Kohlberg saw the values in his research as *the* moral standards.

- The Hindu Advaita Vedanta's idea of justice is that there are no absolute rules, and correct behaviour varies with the role in life you have to play – a priest should not kill, but a soldier should. You do not act for fear of punishment or heavenly reward – you get what you deserve.

- Shintoists believe people are born innocent of evil, so are essentially good. We each have a spirit, so we know right from wrong in our heart, we do not need rules to tell us.

- The aim in Taoism is to preserve life and avoid injury. There are three 'treasures' – compassion, moderation and humility.

- In Buddhism, man is punished by his sins, not for them. An individual's morality develops along the Eightfold Path. Some of the steps of the Path are right views, right thought, right conduct (which includes not taking life, whether human or animal), right livelihood (which includes harming no-one).

Figure 7.5 Compare these beliefs with Kohlberg's six stages

Kohlberg focused on ethical principles such as justice, equality, integrity, reverence for life, which he claimed are universally held. But are they? Research by N. Iwasa (1992) found Americans were most concerned to prolong life (so Heinz should steal the drug) whereas Japanese participants were concerned to make life purer and cleaner (so Heinz should not steal). Children raised on Israeli kibbutzim were more likely to emphasise reciprocity between people, whereas city children (whether from Israel or USA) were more likely to be concerned with the personal costs of helping others.

Methodological bias

Kohlberg has received criticism for the degree to which his research depends on participants being able to express themselves accurately. It can be difficult for people to put their reasoning into words, particularly when they include abstract ideas of justice. It may be no coincidence that those who achieve the higher levels in his classification are also those with better education and higher verbal ability. Those who score lower may have had an intuitive understanding relating to the higher levels, but have been unable to articulate it.

Related to this is a general methodological problem when asking people to give reasons or explanations. In order to categorise their answers (so they can be compared and analysed later), researchers may need to interpret their meanings. The interpretations may be biased and produce biased results. This criticism applies to the work of Piaget, Kohlberg and Gilligan that we have considered in this chapter.

Another fault relates particularly to the dilemmas which Kohlberg presented to his participants. Many of them were unrelated to their lives; indeed, research which has used more life-like dilemmas involving relationships between friends or standards of public behaviour has produced different findings.

Research which underpins social learning theory focuses on behaviour rather than what is said, so it avoids bias in interpreting what is said. However, because it involves **laboratory experiments** such as those conducted by Bandura and his colleagues on aggression (see p.42), the **demand characteristics** may have caused higher levels of imitated behaviour than children would normally show.

In real life, children may be less likely to imitate behaviour because there are a number of conflicting circumstances, some of which we reviewed when we evaluated social learning theory on p.49. Indeed, Bandura noted that some children observed the aggressive behaviour but failed to imitate it. They may have been using moral reasoning to determine whether this behaviour was right or wrong, as indicated by the comment that 'Ladies shouldn't do things like that'.

The OCR exam

The OCR exam will test your ability to:

- demonstrate knowledge and understanding of the theories of Piaget regarding moral development
- demonstrate knowledge and understanding of the theories of Kohlberg regarding moral development
- demonstrate knowledge and understanding of moral development through the behavioural perspective of social learning theory
- consider possible methodological and gender biases in research into moral development, including the work of Gilligan.

Sample exam questions on aspects of morality

1. Explain what is meant by a 'moral dilemma' in psychological research. (2 marks)
2. Describe Piaget's theory of moral development. (4 marks)
3. Explain one disadvantage of the clinical interview method. (2 marks)
4. a Describe another theory of moral development (not Piaget's). (4 marks)
   b Suggest one criticism that can be made of the theory you have described. (2 marks)
5. What is meant by a longitudinal study in psychological research? (2 marks)
6. Identify three types of people which children are likely to imitate, in order to learn right from wrong. (3 marks)
7. Outline Gilligan's criticism of gender bias in research into moral development. (3 marks)

Attitudes of Prejudice

Read the national newspapers or listen to conversations and you will come across people expressing negative attitudes towards others when they have very little information about them. We make assumptions about others simply because we know something of their religion, culture, race, sexual orientation, age, physical appearance or life-style. Why do we do this? In particular, how is it that we can hold negative attitudes towards people we have never met? If we meet them, how do these attitudes affect our behaviour and theirs? This chapter presents some of the answers to these questions which are provided within psychology, and looks at ways in which prejudice and discrimination can be reduced.

Three parts of prejudice

Prejudice can be defined as:

● an attitude towards a particular group or member of the group, based on characteristics which are assumed to be common to all members of the group.

Although prejudice can be positive or negative, it is generally seen as negative and psychologists have been much more concerned with its negative aspects because of the damaging effects. There are three parts of prejudice:

● **Affective** – an attitude composed of negative feelings or emotions towards a group of people.
● **Behavioural** – discrimination against members of a group.
● **Cognitive** – holding stereotyped beliefs and expectations about members of a group.

We examine each of these below, starting with the cognitive part of prejudice.

The cognitive part – stereotyping

A **stereotype** can be defined as:

● a shared belief about the characteristics of those who belong to a particular social or physical category.

Some examples are that black people are good athletes, English people are reserved, people wearing glasses are intelligent. Stereotypes can be positive or negative, but if these traits are negative they form the basis for prejudice.

The stereotype contains very generalised information about members of a group. As we grow up we hear what parents, other adults, peers and people in the media say about members of that group. We do not have to meet a person who belongs to one of these groups, we think we already 'know' about them because we infer that everyone who belongs to the group has these characteristics.

Stereotyping helps us to fill in the gaps in our knowledge about others; unfortunately we tend to fill the gaps with *assumptions* from the stereotype rather than try to find out about that person as an individual. The term **cognitive miser** has been used to describe this type of 'short cut' in thinking. When we think like cognitive misers we fail to make full use of our perceptions and memory. We use the easiest way to make sense of our experiences (such as slotting people into already existing categories) even if we are not always correct or accurate.

'That's the end of the season for him, eh, what?'   'Rather'   'I say old chap, was that you stamping on my face, eh, what?   'Let's not get worked up. It's only a game and all that sort of thing.'

Figure 8.1 These stereotypes about the English come from a French book. At this point in the story the English characters are playing rugby.

When we stereotype someone we tend to notice characteristics consistent with the stereotype and ignore information which does not fit. The stereotype acts like a lens, distorting our view of people so that we interpret ambiguous information in the light of our stereotype.

In a study of how stereotypes can distort our view of others, participants watched a video of two people (who were white and black actors) having a discussion in which one of them pushed the other. **Participants** who saw the black actor doing the pushing rated his behaviour as more violent compared with those who saw the white actor doing the pushing. These results show that participants interpreted the behaviour they saw on the basis of the actor's race. This single feature was enough to affect their judgement.

GROUP ACTIVITY – The characteristics of a stereotype

Each person in your group has a slip of paper and writes down a commonly-held stereotype. On a separate piece of paper, each person now writes down three characteristics on which the stereotype is based. The slip of paper with the stereotype is now passed to someone else. Each member of the group then writes down three characteristics of the new stereotype they have been given. Finally, compare descriptions of the same stereotype: have you written down similar characteristics?

One of the powerful effects of stereotyping is that it leads us to treat people in accordance with our expectations of them. They may then show the behaviour we expect, which proves to us that our expectations were correct. This is an example of the **self-fulfilling prophecy** and is one reason why stereotypes may be difficult to break down once they are created.

The affective part – negative feelings and emotions

Even if we have never met anyone belonging to a particular group, if the stereotype contains negative information we will have negative feelings towards any member of the group. These feelings may include discomfort, embarrassment, fear, apprehension, distaste, dislike or anger. This is not always the case; children for example can provide stereotypical information about a particular group but there is no evidence of dislike or fear when the stereotype contains negative information.

We may also develop negative feelings towards people from a particular group if we hear those around us speaking in a derogatory way, or using an unpleasant tone of voice when talking about them.

The behavioural part – discrimination

Discrimination refers to the way we behave with those we are prejudiced towards, so **discrimination** can be defined as:

● treating someone differently simply because they belong to a particular group.

We may show discrimination by:

● **What we say** – such as telling racist or sexist jokes, being rude to them.
● **How we treat them** – such as avoiding eye contact, or ignoring someone who is in a wheelchair.
● **How we use our personal space** – keeping a greater distance from those we are prejudiced towards.
● **What we do** – attacking them or their property.

Tanni Grey-Thompson won several medals at the Paralympics in 2000 and flying around the world has become part of her everyday life. She has needed a wheelchair since she was seven years old and describes it as her most important thing because it gives her independence. Recalling an incident when the check-in staff at an airport wanted her to leave her own chair and be pushed on board in one of the airport models, she describes her refusal. As the queue lengthened behind her she suggested that the check-in clerk tell all the other people to take off their shoes and socks to go on board. The clerk replied 'We can't do that, it's a personal liberty issue!' 'Precisely,' replied Tanni.

Figure 8.2 A tale of discrimination – Tanni Grey-Thompson

The link between a prejudiced attitude and discrimination is not always direct. A well-known study of **discrimination** was conducted by R. LaPiere (1934) who travelled extensively in the USA with a young Chinese couple. This was at a time of considerable anti-Chinese feeling. In all their visits to hotels and restaurants they experienced discrimination only once.

However, after visiting these establishments LaPiere wrote to them asking about their attitudes to Chinese people. More than 100 replied, and 90 per cent of these said they would not accept Chinese clients. These results can be taken as evidence that prejudice is not directly linked to discrimination, although you may be able to think of other reasons why LaPiere found this discrepancy in his research.

Types of prejudice

There are many types of prejudice; below are some of the most common:

- **Sexism** – discrimination on the grounds of sex, including a belief in the superiority of one's own sex and inferiority of the other sex. Sexism originally referred to male attitudes towards women, but the term is now used to refer to any discrimination on the basis of sex.
- **Heterosexism** – regarding gay men and lesbian women as abnormal and discriminating against them on the basis of their sexual orientation.

- **Racism** – a negative attitude towards someone of another race, contrasted with feelings of superiority about one's own race. It is illegal to show racism, but it still exists within society. For example, a cross-cultural study carried out in Holland and America looked at how racism is communicated between whites. In the wider society there was a **social norm** not to show racism, but within various sub-groups (such as the family, in the workplace, amongst neighbours) racist talk and behaviour was acceptable. This suggests that challenging racism at the official level will not eliminate it. Racism, or indeed any form of prejudice and discrimination, needs to be tackled at the unofficial level as well, which means the individual refusing to conform to social norms and challenging others when they show racism.

- **Ethnocentrism** – a belief in the superiority of your own cultural group, a tendency to see everything from the point of view of your own group. Kohlberg (see Kohlberg's theory of moral development, p.89) was accused of ethnocentrism in his categorisation of moral principles because he gave the highest value to principles rated most highly in the West.
- **Ageism** – discrimination on the basis of age, making assumptions about a person's abilities and interests simply because of their age.

Causes of prejudice

Psychologists have suggested several possible causes of prejudice. Below we look at three explanations.

The authoritarian personality

The notion that prejudice can be due to a personality type was proposed by T. Adorno (1950) in America. In his research to find an explanation for the behaviour of Nazi soldiers in World War II he interviewed and tested hundreds of people. He and his colleagues found a particular pattern of personality character-istics which they called the **authoritarian personality**. Those with an authoritarian personality tend to be:

- hostile to those who are of inferior status
- obedient and servile to those of higher status
- fairly rigid in their opinions and beliefs
- intolerant of uncertainty or ambiguity
- conventional, upholding traditional values.

Those with an authoritarian personality were more likely to have had a very strict upbringing by critical and harsh parents. Adorno claimed that they experienced unconscious hostility towards their parents which they were unable to express towards them. This hostility was **displaced** (see p.40), and was redirected to those who were weaker and so unable to hurt them.

Evaluation of the authoritarian personality explanation

This notion of the authoritarian personality corresponds to the hostility towards minority groups which is found in prejudice; however, it is only a correlation. It could be that children learned these behaviours through observation and imitation of their parents – through **social learning**. Adorno's claim that the authoritarian personality is caused by a particular style of parenting does not seem to be widely applicable, because not all prejudiced people had harsh parents. Indeed, some prej-udiced people show few features of the authoritarian personality, which should not be the case according to this explanation.

Finally, there is evidence that prejudice towards minority groups increases in times of hardship, which the authoritarian personality theory can not explain. A better explanation comes from the idea of competition for scarce resources (see p.104).

Social identity theory

One of the basic cognitive processes is categorisation, the tendency to group things together. Several psychologists have proposed that we divide people into two basic groups – the in-group ('us') and the out-group ('them').

H. Tajfel (1971) called this **social categorisation** and it is the first step in the stereotyping process. He showed that not only do we categorise people but we **discriminate** against members of the out-group. Tajfel and others have found that:

- **We favour the in-group over the out-group** – in other words, we discriminate. We think members of the out-group are less attractive, less intelligent, less able and so on. When our group fails it is due to bad luck, when the other group fails it is because they are not very good.
- **We exaggerate the differences** between the in-group and the out-group.
- **We see the members of the out-group as more alike** than they really are, which is reflected in comments such as 'They're all the same, these youngsters' or 'Those Japanese all look alike to me.'

Why do we do this? In their **social identity theory**, H. Tajfel and J. Turner (1986) argue that membership of our group – our psychology class, football team,

Figure 8.3 Are members of the same group as alike as we tend to think?

neighbourhood and so on – is an important source of pride and self-esteem. We increase our self-esteem by enhancing the status of the group to which we belong (the in-group) and denigrating the out-group. The more we need to raise our self-esteem, the more we are likely to denigrate the out-group, and this explains why some people are more prejudiced than others.

Evaluation of the social identity theory explanation

Social identity theory explains why large numbers of people may be prejudiced towards particular groups, and why some people are more prejudiced than others. The tendency to discriminate is less evident in societies which stress co-operation between people, which indicates that social attitudes play an important role, as social identity theory recognises.

However, critics argue that Tajfel's evidence is based largely on **experimental** work which is artificial; in real life we enhance our own group, but it seems we do not necessarily denigrate others.

Competition

Prejudice has been explained as due to competition which exists between various groups in society. This may be political or economic competition, and is most intense when resources are limited. For example, research has shown that between 1880 and 1930 in the US, failures in the cotton crop (leading to harsh economic conditions) correlated with an increase in the lynchings of black Americans. So, when resources such as jobs, homes, land or water are scarce there may be an increase in prejudice towards other groups.

Muzafer Sherif devised a **field experiment** to study the role of competition and co-operation in inter-group relations. Sherif and colleagues (1961) observed the behaviour of 12-year-old boys who were attending a summer camp in America called The Robber's Cave. The 22 participants were not known to each other and all were white, psychologically well-adjusted and from stable middle-class homes.

They were **randomly** assigned to two groups but neither was aware of the other's existence. For a few days normal summer camp activities took place and both groups quickly established their own culture – naming themselves the 'Rattlers' and the 'Eagles' and developing **group norms**.

Then a series of inter-group contests was devised by the counsellors, who promised a trophy for the winning group. In addition, situations were devised in which one group gained at the expense of the other: for example, one group was delayed getting to a picnic and when they arrived the other group had eaten most of the food. Hostility quickly arose, groups derided and attacked each other. Each group became more united, and the more aggressive boys became leaders.

At the end of the competitions joint social events were arranged to increase contact between the groups, but observers noted that hostility did not decrease. These results suggest that competition increases prejudice and discrimination towards the out-group and increases unity of the in-group. Also, contact with members of the out-group does not appear to reduce prejudice and discrimination.

Evaluation of the inter-group competition explanation

This explanation is supported by evidence that people living in more competitive cultures show higher levels of discrimination than people in co-operative cultures. There is research evidence to suggest that in times of economic hardship there are increasing levels of prejudice and discrimination. We have also seen that group norms can be a powerful influence on behaviour (see Conformity, pp.8–9).

There are some methodological criticisms which undermine the researchers' conclusions, however, namely:

- **These groups were artificial**, as were the competitions, and so they did not necessarily reflect real life.
- **The results cannot be generalised** because the research used 12-year-old boys and excluded, for example, girls and adults.
- **The research raises ethical concerns** because it permitted and possibly encouraged hostility and aggression between participants. Some of the boys may have been distressed by this, as well as by the situations the researchers devised.

There was a final stage in this experiment, which is described under Increasing co-operation (see p.106).

How can prejudice be reduced?

Prejudice is damaging to a society, as well as being unjust, which is why psychologists have studied ways of reducing it. Success in reducing prejudice depends on the cause. For example, it has been argued that those with an **authoritarian personality** are unlikely to change their attitudes because these are necessary for the release of their hostility. Nevertheless, several strategies for reducing prejudice have been proposed and tested. Three of these are examined below.

Challenging stereotypes

If we can show that stereotypes do not 'fit' reality, they may weaken and so prejudice and discrimination may be reduced. S. Bem (1983) has shown how strong a stereotype can be in her work on gender, and points out that parents have an important role in counteracting stereotypes and in identifying to children when stereotypes are being portrayed in the media. Adults can also draw attention to information which shows that the stereotype does not fit: for example, challenging the male stereotype by saying 'Look how that man is crying, he must be very unhappy'.

The media play an important role in shaping our attitudes, and they therefore have a role in challenging stereotypes. For example, they can:

- **Positively portray** members of stereotyped groups in positions of achievement, responsibility or expertise, to counteract the negative information in the stereotype. Examples could be a disabled university lecturer, a black college principal or a female judge.
- **Increase the exposure** of people who do not fit the stereotype, because the more frequently information conflicts with a stereotype, the more likely it is to weaken. Examples would include a male nurse or a deaf musician.

Figure 8.4 When members of minority groups are seen in positions of authority, this may counteract negative information in a stereotype

According to the **self-fulfilling prophecy**, when the targets of prejudice behave as expected, the perceiver's stereotype is likely to be confirmed. But if the victims of prejudice challenge the other person's expectation, rather than conforming to it, this may break the cycle of the self-fulfilling prophecy. This has been one of the

GROUP ACTIVITY – Reducing prejudice

Several of the photographs in this book have been chosen because they show people in non-stereotypical roles. Find one of them and identify which aspects of the stereotype are challenged in the photograph. Then imagine that as a group you have to produce a TV programme which aims to reduce prejudice by challenging stereotypes. Devise a programme to reduce prejudice towards members of the group shown in the photograph. Use the material in this chapter to give you ideas about what strategies might work, and say how you would put them into effect in the programme.

aims of social movements such as the Black Power, Feminist and Gay Liberation movements in recent decades, who have worked to increase the assertiveness and self-confidence of their members and so halt the self-fulfilling prophecy cycle.

Increasing co-operation

We saw earlier that in Sherif's Robber's Cave experiment simple contact was not enough to reduce hostility between groups. In the 1970s E. Aronson noted that there had always been contact between black and white Americans, yet prejudice and discrimination had not reduced. One possible solution is to bring together those who are prejudiced in order to co-operate in joint tasks.

This is what Sherif did in the final stage of the experiment: all the boys had to co-operate on tasks such as pulling a truck back to camp in order to get there in time for lunch. These are called tasks with superordinate goals, which means that they require everyone's input in order to be achieved. After several of these, the inter-group hostility disappeared.

It seems that co-operation reduces prejudice, but this conclusion has been criticised because:

- **All the boys were fairly similar**, while the groups and hostility were artificially created. Real life is different – there are *physical* differences between people which make them easy to categorise, there may be **social norms** supporting prejudice and there may be differences in social status between groups. Simple co-operation in these circumstances is not enough, and these other factors also need to be tackled if prejudice is to be reduced.
- **Co-operating on tasks brings mixed results**. This is illustrated in an American study which arranged for very prejudiced white and black people to work together on a series of joint tasks. Results showed that six months later 40 per cent of the participants were much less prejudiced, 40 per cent had not changed their attitudes and 20 per cent had become *more* prejudiced.

● **Higher status members dominate** when members of two groups are in contact. Research shows that they tend to initiate things, be listened to by others, and their views are more likely to be followed. To reduce prejudice through joint tasks, those who are the victims of prejudice must be of higher status (having better jobs or a higher level of education) in order to change the attitudes of those who are prejudiced.

Figure 8.5 Increasing the contact between races may not be sufficient because those of higher status may dominate

Creating empathy

If we experience the effects of prejudice and discrimination, we might try to change our attitudes. J. Elliott (1977) told her class of nine-year-olds that brown-eyed people were better and more intelligent than those with blue eyes, and should therefore be given extra privileges. The children started to behave according to these stereotypes: the brown-eyed became more dominant and produced better work, the blue-eyed became angry or depressed and their work deteriorated. The next day she told them she was wrong and that blue-eyed people were superior: the patterns of behaviour quickly reversed.

On the third day she told them the truth, that there were no such differences but that she wanted them to feel what it was like to be judged on the basis of one, irrelevant, physical feature which they could not change: in other words, to feel the effects of **stereotyping**. This helped them to understand how stereotyping caused **prejudice** and **discrimination**, and how unpleasant and unfair it was. Helping people to empathise like this can be an effective strategy for the reduction of prejudice and discrimination in children and adults.

The OCR exam

The OCR exam will test your ability to:

- define prejudice and show an awareness of the affective (attitudinal), behavioural (discriminatory) and cognitive (stereotyping) component parts of prejudice
- be aware of prejudice including sexism, ethnocentrism, racism, ageism
- describe and evaluate different theoretical causes of prejudice, e.g. personality (Adorno), social identity theory (Tajfel)
- describe possible means of reducing prejudice, e.g. group co-operation (Sherif).

Sample exam questions on attitudes of prejudice

1. Identify two types of prejudice. (1+1 mark)
2. Give a definition of prejudice. (2 marks)
3. Name the three component parts of prejudice. (3 marks)
4. Describe one example of discrimination in everyday life. (2 marks)
5. a Describe one theory of prejudice, e.g. Adorno's personality theory, Tajfel's social identity theory. (4 marks)
   b Give one criticism of this theory. (2 marks)
6. Explain one way of reducing prejudice. (4 marks)

Cognitive Psychology

Cognitive psychology aims to understand the internal mental processes involved in interpreting and making sense of the world around us. This is illustrated in the next two chapters.

Chapter 9 looks at some aspects of Memory, including why we forget and how we can improve remembering. Chapter 10 looks at Perception, in particular how we make sense of what we see – visual perception.

Memory

Without memory we would be unable to do many of the things we take for granted, to use words, to dress ourselves, to recognise a familiar voice, even to recognise our own face in the mirror. Without memory, everything we experience would seem to be experienced for the first time; it would be completely new to us. As well as giving a background to some of the work on memory, this chapter considers reasons why we forget and some ideas for helping us remember, which is particularly useful for students who are about to sit exams!

The stages of memory

When you are watching a film your brain has to process the information you receive from it. The images you see enter your eyes as light waves, what you hear enters your ears as sound waves. In order that you can make use of it, this information goes through the following three stages.

Encoding

Information is changed (or encoded) so that we can make sense of it. Light waves are converted into images (see Perceptual abilities, p.125), sound waves are converted into words, words are converted into meanings. Once encoded, the information can be **stored**.

Storage

The information that has been **encoded** is then stored, so it is available for use at some time in the future. Our memory for a word will include memory for what it sounds like, what it looks like and what it means. We store different types of information in different ways, as you will see shortly, and the way we store information affects how we **retrieve** it.

Retrieval

This occurs when we try to recover information from storage. If we 'can't remember' something, it may be because we are unable to **retrieve** it. This happens when you go to pick up something from another room, but when you get there cannot remember what you have gone for. Returning to the original room often enables you to retrieve the information. Sometimes we really think we have forgotten something, perhaps how to do something on a computer. Then someone shows us what to do, and after only one demonstration we can remember the whole sequence. This is called **re-learning** – we seem to have almost remembered what to do but need a little extra help to remember it completely.

Atkinson and Shiffrin's two-process theory

One of the first psychologists, W. James (1890), distinguished between **short-term memory** and **long-term memory**. This distinction forms the basis for the model described below, which has been widely used as a framework for research.

The key features of Atkinson and Shiffrin's model

R. Atkinson and R. Shiffrin (1968) proposed that we pay attention to some of the information which is registered by the senses, and that the rest is lost through decay. This incoming **sensory information** passes into short-term memory.

Only a small amount of information can be held in short-term memory: up to about seven items, so new information coming in pushes out (or **displaces**) information already held. Information can only be held in short-term memory for up to 30 seconds, but if it is **rehearsed** then it transfers to long-term memory. Here it may remain indefinitely and can be retrieved for future use.

As you can see in Figure 9.1, the key features in this model are therefore incoming sensory information, short-term memory, displacement, rehearsal, transfer, long-term memory and retrieval.

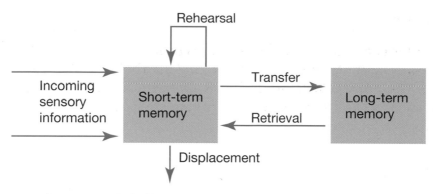

Figure 9.1 Atkinson and Shiffrin's model of memory

The main differences between short-term and long-term memory

You may recall that at the start of the chapter we noted that information goes through three stages in memory: encoding, storage and retrieval. In Atkinson and Shiffrin's model, information goes through these three stages in both short- and then long-term memory. A comparison of short- and long-term memory, in terms of these stages, is shown below in Table 9.1.

Stages	Short-term memory	Long-term memory
Encoding	Mainly acoustic (as heard) or visual (as seen)	Mainly semantic (by meaning) or acoustic or visual
Storage Capacity Duration	7 (+ or – 2 items) Up to 30 seconds	Unlimited From minutes to years
Retrieval	Only possible immediately, information is retrieved in original form	Possible any time, can use links with other material to retrieve, information may be different each time retrieved

Table 9.1 A comparison of short- and long-term memory

Evaluation of Atkinson and Shiffrin's model

Although the model (see Figure 9.1) does provide a simple description of memory processes and research supports the characteristics of **short-** and **long-term** memory described above, it has been widely criticised for its focus on memory for new facts, such as word lists, numbers or nonsense syllables. This is why the model seems to explain how we remember a telephone number until we can dial it, but it cannot explain many of our everyday experiences of memory.

For instance, why are we able to recall information which we did not rehearse, yet are unable to recall information which we have rehearsed? Why can we remember how to swim, which is not learned as 'pieces' of information? Why could you read this page several times and yet recall very little of it? Because Atkinson and Shiffrin's model cannot provide satisfactory answers to these questions, researchers have explored a number of other possible explanations. We will look briefly at two models which have been developed as a result of criticism of the Atkinson and Shiffrin model.

Figure 9.2 How can Atkinson and Shiffrin's model be used to explain how this athlete remembers her skills?

In 1974 A. Baddeley and G. Hitch criticised the idea that short-term memory was simply a store for information being transferred to or from long-term memory. Their research showed that **participants** were able to retain seven numbers whilst doing a simple reasoning task, thus suggesting that there are several sub-systems within **short-term memory** which include memories for visual, spoken and written information. They proposed the idea of **working memory**, rather than a simple store, because of the various types of memory and the tasks that could be performed.

Criticism of Atkinson and Shiffrin's proposal of memory stores has also come from psychologists who argue that what is important is the processing rather than the storage of information. F. Craik and R. Lockhart (1972) showed that participants who had to work out the meaning of a word were more likely to recall it than those who had simply to say whether it was written in capital or lower-case letters. Why was recall better? They answer that it is because the information was processed in a deeper (or more complex) way, which they called **elaboration**. This is called the **levels of processing** approach, and provides a better explanation of some of our everyday experiences of memory. When we look at ways of improving memory (pp.121–4), you will see that every technique involves elaboration of the material.

> ## GROUP ACTIVITY – The three stages of memory
>
> In pairs, analyse each of the following presentations of information in terms of encoding, storage and retrieval. Using Atkinson and Shiffrin's model, try to describe how the information is encoded, explain how it becomes stored in long-term memory and how you might retrieve it.
>
> 1 A friend's description of a film they have just seen.
> 2 The diagram in Figure 9.1.
> 3 Your first day at school.
>
> Compare your analysis with analyses from the other pairs. What difficulties did you have trying to fit your explanation to Atkinson and Shiffrin's model?

Theories of forgetting

There are many reasons why we 'forget', although it is difficult to test them because we may not in fact forget, we may be unable to retrieve the memory from storage. These theories of forgetting are therefore also possible explanations for why we seem to be unable to retrieve a memory, or why that memory is distorted.

Interference theory

Our memory may be hampered by information we have already stored, or by new experiences which occur whilst we are taking in the information. There are two types of interference:

● **Retroactive interference** occurs when information you receive later interferes with your ability to recall something you learned earlier. This could happen to someone who knows some Spanish and then starts learning Italian. If they try to speak Spanish they may find they are only able to remember words in the new language – Italian.

● **Proactive interference** occurs when something you already know interferes with your ability to take in new information. If you go into your local supermarket and the goods have been rearranged, you will continue to go to the 'old' place for your crisps, even after several visits. Another example comes from **stereotyping**, where information you already have about someone prevents you from taking in new (and different) information about them (see Stereotyping, pp.98–9).

Evaluation of interference theory

Interference theory is a possible explanation for some of the examples given above, but with proactive interference in particular it is often possible to 'remember' with just a little effort. In the supermarket as you approach the crisps shelf and see it holds toilet rolls, you will probably be able to recall where the crisps have been moved to. The information has been stored but it was inaccessible.

Another criticism of interference theory is that it is based on **laboratory experiments** requiring participants to remember words. This is a rather limited test of forgetting, so the results may not reflect real life very well.

Motivated forgetting

In his psychoanalytic theory, Sigmund Freud (1901) proposed that when we find an experience very distressing we push it down into our unconscious so that we cannot access it, which he called **repression**. Our **ego**, which is conscious, manages our unconscious desires and constraints so that we can function in everyday life (see p.40 for more details). We must defend our ego from excessive anxiety, so we use **ego defence mechanisms** and one of these is repression, which helps us cope with strong emotional feelings. Distressing memories may not be completely repressed; part of the memory may be accessible to the individual, or the memory may be distorted.

Evaluation of motivated forgetting

Psychoanalytic techniques (such as dream interpretation) can be used to access repressed memories but they may produce quite distressing feelings in the individual, which raises **ethical** concerns. If the individual is very upset by these memories, they may be buried so deeply that they cannot be accessed.

For ethical reasons the traumatic experiences of participants cannot be manipulated in a laboratory, nor can participants be subjected to very **distressing** or anxiety-provoking experiments. One possible source of information is work done with patients suffering from post-traumatic stress disorder, but this is subject to **confidentiality** and its main purpose is to help the patient, not to gain information. Any conclusions drawn cannot be **generalised** to the whole population because they are based on work with one person – a **case study**.

This is why it has proved difficult to gather experimental evidence for repression and may be one of the reasons why research sometimes produces conflicting results. As an example, a study of memory for anxiety-producing words compared with neutral words found that participants recalled fewer anxiety-producing words immediately after learning them, but four weeks later they could recall *more* anxiety-producing words than neutral ones.

Other critics argue that we forget unpleasant or disturbing experiences because of the stress they cause, not because of repression. If we are frightened or angry, for example, our bodily responses change to cope with the situation (see Stress, pp.144–5). These changes interfere with our cognitive abilities, so we may forget because we are unable to process the information properly. According to Atkinson and Shiffrin's model the incoming sensory information may be disrupted, information may not be **rehearsed**, it may **decay** and so fail to pass into long-term memory.

Retrieval failure

A common reason for forgetting is that we cannot retrieve information which we have stored. Perhaps you just cannot recall the title of a film when you are talking with friends, but later when you are brushing your teeth it comes to you. You have not forgotten the information, you just could not retrieve it when you wanted to.

It seems as if we have so much information stored that we cannot always access it, but research shows that if we recall something which is associated with the information, this acts as a **cue** and recall may follow. Let us look at three types of cue.

- **Context-dependent** cues are those related to the situation where new material was learned. For example, participants given a list of words to learn in a basement room recalled an average of 18 words when tested there next day. However, others who recalled in an upper room with completely different furnishings averaged 12 words. A third group was tested in the upper room but advised to imagine being in the basement, and their recall averaged 17. Try imagining yourself back in the classroom if you cannot remember something in your examinations, because the context may act as a retrieval cue.
- **State-dependent** cues refer to retrieving information which you learned when in a particular mood or condition. Research suggests that if participants were sad, happy or drunk when a memory was created, their recall was better if they were in the same mood or condition when trying to retrieve the information.

- **Semantic** cues are those which have a similar meaning to the information which is to be retrieved. In a **laboratory experiment** by G. Bousfield (1953), participants were given 60 words to recall. The words came from four categories (animals, professions, names and vegetables) but were presented in a random order. Results showed that participants recalled words in clusters from the same category, suggesting that we spontaneously organise information by meaning. Other research has shown that participants remember more words if they are organised by meaning, as compared with participants who see them presented **randomly**. When we look at ways of improving memory, you will see that organisation is a useful strategy.

Evaluation of retrieval failure

These effects are not always strong; so, for example, context may have little influence if it is not relevant to what we are doing. Another problem is that much of the supporting evidence is from **laboratory experiments** which may not reflect real life very well.

In contrast, one of the strengths of this explanation is that it is relevant to everyday life. An example of context improving retrieval is when you can only remember what you went downstairs for if you go back to the room where you first thought about it. The everyday use of cues has been found in research, because it seems that being in the same mood may improve retrieval of personal memories more than it improves memory of words in lists. This is one of the reasons why context and mood are sometimes incorporated by police officers in their interviews of eyewitnesses.

GROUP ACTIVITY – Using memory

Read through this sample of questions which help to diagnose Alzheimer's disease (a disease which includes memory loss).

1 What city are we in?
2 What is your date of birth?
3 Name three objects. (Ask the person to repeat them until he or she has learned all three, if possible. Note how long this takes).
4 Spell WORLD forwards and backwards.
5 What were the three objects you named a few minutes ago?
6 Will you please take a paper in your right hand, fold it in half, and put it on the floor.

Working with a partner, look through the questions to see if you can find an example of each of the following:
 retrieval from long-term memory
 evidence of retroactive interference
 rehearsal
 use of short-term memory.

Trace decay theory

According to this theory, information is forgotten as time passes. The memory trace involves tiny changes in the brain, and if the memory is to be retained this trace must be strengthened, which is what happens in **rehearsal**. Unless it is strengthened, the trace decays, i.e. it breaks down and fades. This is an explanation for memory loss in short-term memory but it has also been used to explain some long-term memory loss, in so far as lack of use of information in long-term memory may also lead to decay of the memory trace.

Evaluation of trace decay theory

One of the strengths of trace decay theory is that it explains **re-learning** (see p.114). It is as if going through something just once or twice strengthens a memory that had started to decay. However, the prediction that the memory trace fades over time was tested in an **experiment** by J. Jenkins and K. Dallenbach (1924). Participants were asked to learn a list of nonsense syllables, and then half of the participants slept and the other half stayed awake. If time is the main factor, then recall should have been equally good for both groups. In fact, it was better in the group which slept, which suggests that it is not time which causes decay but what happens *during* the time.

We cannot know whether information really is forgotten or whether we are simply unable to **retrieve** it. For example, something might trigger a memory which you thought you had forgotten. Without that particular cue you might never have recalled it, it would apparently be 'forgotten'. Another weakness in the theory is that some memories do not decay even though they may be very rarely used, such as the knowledge of how to swim or ride a bike.

Improving memory

From the vast amount of research on memory, psychologists have been able to suggest techniques to help people improve their memory. These techniques, known as **mnemonics** (or memory aids), usually require working with the material to be remembered or linking it with material already in long-term memory. This aids in the **encoding** of new material and in its **retrieval**, so it is obviously helpful for students who want to remember the material they are studying. Below we look at several techniques.

Organisation in memory

Material is remembered better if it is organised in a logical or structured way. By organising the material consciously, you have to think about it first. This additional **processing** helps retain the information, and organising it requires the making of links between parts of the material. Both aspects of organisation therefore help improve the memory of the material. Some examples of organisation are:

● **Hierarchical organisation** – starting with a general category which is then divided into several sub-categories, which are in turn subdivided into more specific information. For example, the headings in every chapter of this book are hierarchical, as you can see in the Group Activity below.

> ### GROUP ACTIVITY – Creating hierarchies
>
> Working in pairs, complete the hierarchy of headings in this chapter, as shown in Figure 9.3 below. When you have done that, compare notes so that you are confident you have inserted the correct heading in the right place. You can then insert another layer of sub-divisions at the bottom of the hierarchy. For example, under the topic of 'interference' you can add the three sub-divisions of 'retroactive', 'proactive' and 'evaluation'.
>
> As a revision exercise, in pairs, create your own hierarchy of the topics in other chapters of the book.

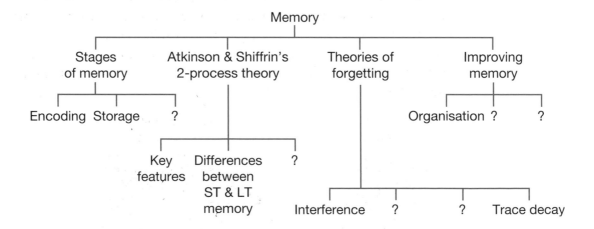

Figure 9.3 Complete this hierarchical diagram of the headings in this chapter. This should help you understand and remember the material in this chapter.

- **Mapping** – if you create a mind map you can see all the aspects of a topic and how they are related to each other visually. You can use this instead of a hierarchy when it is not possible to divide the material into neat subdivisions. If you turn to p.26 you will see a mind map for the information in Chapter 2 on Environment and Behaviour. Make your own mind maps for other chapters.
- **In a sequence**, such as alphabetically, or by size or by time. Imagine a patient discharged from hospital whose treatment involved taking various pills at different times, changing a dressing and doing exercises. If the doctor gives these instructions in the order in which they must be carried out through the day, this will help the patient remember them.

Imagery

Research shows that we remember information better if we can also form an image of it. This may be because it enables us to make a link with information we already know, but also because it ties together two types of information, that which is verbal (spoken or written) and that which is visual. Some examples of the use of imagery to help recall are:

- **Method of loci** uses a familiar place or route as a link with a list of things to be recalled. In order to remember a shopping list you could imagine your route to the shops and create an image of each item, such as bread going in the bank, tomatoes at the traffic lights, sugar in the school playground, biscuits on the building site. You might notice in this example that the item and the place begin with the same letter. Using sound and rhythm is an additional aid to memory. Method of loci also organises material in a **sequence**, which is another memory aid, described on the previous page under Organisation in memory.
- **Linking an image with a word** – when learning a new language, the learner creates an image which sounds like the new word. Figure 9.4 shows some examples you could use when learning French.

Five is 'CINQ'
(pronounced sank)

Wine is 'VIN'
(pronounced van)

Figure 9.4 Examples of the use of imagery when learning French

Rehearsal

This idea of rehearsal is a key feature of the Atkinson and Shiffrin model, where we saw that information passes from short- to long-term memory if it is rehearsed. One reason for forgetting is **decay** of the memory trace (see pp.121), so if we repeat information when it is new, then we strengthen the memory trace so we should be more likely to remember it.

Rehearsal is used throughout this book to help you remember information. You will see that topics such as ethics, research methods (for example case studies, experiments, interviews) and new terms (behaviour, cognitive, innate and so on) occur in several places. Although they are explained in detail at one point, the fact that they are repeated in other contexts should help you recall them.

The OCR exam

The OCR exam will test your ability to:

● show awareness of the encoding, storage and retrieval stages of memory
● show knowledge and understanding of Atkinson and Shiffrin's two-process theory
● describe and evaluate theories of forgetting, e.g. interference, motivated forgetting
● demonstrate knowledge and understanding of the use of organisation and imagery in aiding memory (mnemonics) applications, e.g. study skills.

Sample exam questions on memory

1. Explain what is meant by the term 'encoding' in relation to memory. (2 marks)
2. Explain the main features of Atkinson and Shiffrin's two process theory. (5 marks)
3. a What was the method used in Bousfield's study (p.120)? (1 mark)
   b Explain one advantage and one disadvantage of this method of research. (2+2 marks)
4. a Describe one theory of forgetting. (4 marks)
   b Give one criticism of this theory. (2 marks)
5. a Name one technique for improving memory. (1 mark)
   b Explain how this technique works. (3 marks)

Perception

P erception is the process of interpreting, organising and elaborating on sensory information. So when we study visual perception we look at how we make sense of the information which comes into our brain through our eyes. As you look at this page, light waves enter your eye, but it is your visual perception which enables you to organise them into a pattern of black and white marks which you understand as letter shapes. Psychologists have investigated the extent to which visual perception develops as a result of our experiences, or whether most of our visual abilities are innate. This is a major theme of this chapter.

Perceptual abilities

The sensory information for vision is light waves, which enter the eye, strike the retina at the back of the eye and are then changed into electrical impulses which are transmitted to the brain. Our focus in this chapter is how we make sense of this information – how we interpret it, how we organise and elaborate on it. We look first at visual constancies, then perception of depth and finally some visual illusions.

Visual constancies

As we move about in our world, and as the objects we look at move about, the sensory information we receive is constantly changing but what we see does not seem to change to the same extent. This is because our perceptual abilities make adjustments to this sensory information, as you can see below.

Size constancy

If somebody walks towards you, the image they create on your retina will get larger but they do not appear to grow bigger because your **perception** has made adjustments to the sensory information. This is an example of **size constancy**. In Figure 10.1a the further figure appears larger than she actually is (Figure 10.1b shows a comparison). Why is this? In the first photograph we do not see the woman's size as different from the woman in front, rather we see her distance from the front woman. The perspective lines in the corridor indicate distance, so our perception 'scales up' the image to compensate for the distance.

Size constancy does not always occur; if you look at oncoming vehicles through a car windscreen, they *do* appear to grow much larger in size. The windscreen provides a frame of reference with which your perception compares the changing size of the vehicles.

Figure 10.1a Women sitting in a corridor

Figure 10.1b The two figures in Figure 10.1a side by side

Shape constancy

When you lift a mug to your lips the image of its shape alters: for example, the top becomes a full circle as you tip it. Although the information you receive about its shape changes, you perceive it as unchanged: this is an example of **shape constancy**. In Figure 10.2 the shape of the door changes as it opens, yet we do not see it as changing shape but as changing its position.

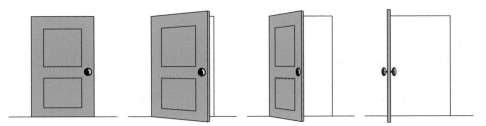

Figure 10.2 Shape constancy – the opening door

Colour constancy

The redness of a tomato seems the same whether we see it in bright sunshine or deep shade; this is an example of **colour constancy**. We judge colour by comparing an object with the intensity of the colours surrounding it and we make allowances for the difference in light, so we perceive the tomato's colour as similar, regardless of its actual appearance. Try this in the group activity described below.

> ### GROUP ACTIVITY – Demonstrating colour constancy
>
> Gather a number of smallish coloured objects, for example, an apple, orange, watch strap, lipstick case, as well as a cardboard tube (perhaps the centre of a paper-towel roll). Place one of the objects on a well-lit surface and look at it through the cardboard tube so the object appears to 'fill' the end of the tube. Whilst you are looking at it, ask someone else to create shade over the object. Note how the colour of the object appears to change.
>
> Now repeat this without using the cardboard tube. You will see how the change in colour is much less apparent, because you perceive the colour of the object in relation to its surroundings. Try this with the other objects you have assembled.

Depth perception

The image that falls on the retina is two-dimensional, so how can we see the world in three dimensions, how do we perceive depth? We do this by using information from both eyes (binocular cues) or one eye (monocular cues).

Binocular depth cues

● **Binocular disparity** – because each eye looks at the world from a slightly different point, we get two slightly different views of an object. Try this yourself by holding a pencil at arm's length, closing one eye and lining the pencil up against the window or a corner of the room. Now close this eye and open the other; the pencil 'jumps' to one side. This is because you are seeing it from a different point – from your other eye. With both eyes open, the brain is receiving these two different sets of information. The brain integrates this information and we perceive the object three-dimensionally.

● **Ocular convergence** – the nearer an object is, the more the eyes turn inward (converge) in order to see that object. Information passes from the eye muscles to the brain, telling the brain how much the eyes have turned and helping us to perceive how close, or far away, an object is.

Monocular depth cues

We can still perceive depth using only one eye because of visual cues in our environment. We seem to learn these from experience, and these cues are also used to show depth (three dimensions) in pictures (which are two-dimensional), as shown in Figure 10.3.

Overlap – if one object hides part of another, the complete object is closer

Height in the visual field – the closer to the horizon the object is, the further away it is

Relative size – larger objects are closer

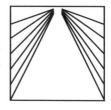

Linear perspective – parallel lines converge as they recede into the distance

Texture gradient – the texture or gradient becomes finer as it gets further away

Figure 10.3 Some monocular cues for depth perception

Illusions

In visual illusions our perception seems to play tricks on us, because of the way it interprets the information which the eyes receive. These three examples are shown in Figure 10.4:

- **The Ponzo illusion** – The image on the retina is of two horizontal lines of equal length, yet we perceive the higher line as longer than the lower one. This could be because the converging lines give perspective cues, so we 'scale up' the higher line, which also occurs in Figure 10.1a.
- **The Müller–Lyer illusion** – Both these lines are of equal length on the retinal image, yet we perceive the one with the outgoing fins as longer.
- **The Necker cube** – If you look at the coloured face on the cube it will eventually appear to jump and the configuration of the cube changes – this is called depth reversal. The image on the retina is a two-dimensional line drawing but we

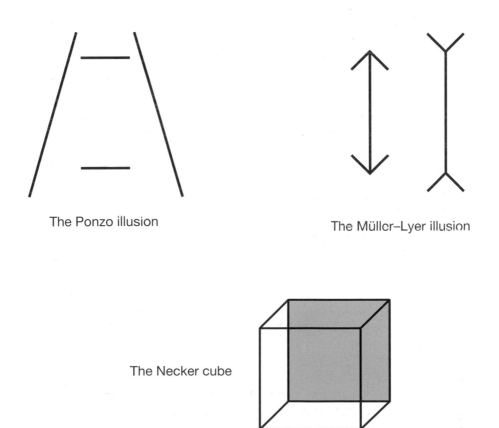

The Ponzo illusion

The Müller–Lyer illusion

The Necker cube

Figure 10.4 Three visual illusions

perceive a three-dimensional cube. We cannot see both configurations of the cube at once and we seem to be unable to control when the change occurs.

Perceptual abilities – nature or nuture

Some psychologists studying the development of our perceptual abilities have tried to discover whether these abilities are innate or learned:

- **Innate** abilities are those we are born with: some may be evident at birth but the development of others depends largely on maturation – this represents the 'nature' view of development.
- **Learned** abilities develop through our experiences – this represents the 'nurture' view of development.

You will see as we review and assess the evidence for these two perspectives that psychologists have used a variety of methods, all of which pose difficulties for the researcher. We will start with a consideration of perceptual abilities that may be innate.

The role of nature

To find out which visual abilities are **innate**, psychologists have to eliminate the effect of the environment. One way of doing this is to study the newborn infant; another is to find out whether perceptual abilities develop in people who have been blind from birth but gain sight as adults. These are called deprivation studies. Research using these two approaches is described below.

Infant (neonate) studies

Testing babies is complicated because they may be sleepy, bored, unwell or slow to respond to stimuli. These difficulties are reduced as the baby gets older, but by then the environment will have started to have an impact on their development. In addition, because babies cannot tell us what they see, we can only infer their abilities or understanding from their behaviour. Nevertheless, researchers have found that newborns can:

- focus on objects approximately 20 cm away, but cannot vary this focal length
- differentiate between light and dark, because they look at (fixate) on the *edge* of objects, which are defined by the contrast between light and dark
- differentiate between an object and its background, because if an infant fixates on an object which is then moved slowly, its eyes follow the movement.

These abilities are present at birth and so are likely to be innate, but as you will see below, more complex abilities seem to appear a little later. These may be due to **maturation** (which means they are innate) or to experience.

Form or pattern perception

The ability to recognise pattern was investigated in a series of laboratory experiments by R. Fantz (1961). He presented two different patterns side by side to infants between one and 15 weeks of age, and measured how much time the baby looked at each of them. His aim was to find out whether the infants spent more time looking at the more complex pattern. The results of his research showed they did (see Figure 10.5). Fantz concluded that because infants could perceive pattern very soon after birth this ability is likely to be **innate**, since it could not have been **learned**.

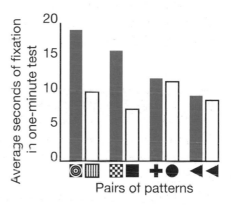

Figure 10.5 Bar chart showing amount of fixation time for each pattern

GROUP ACTIVITY – Infants' visual abilities

From the results shown in Figure 10.5, Fantz concluded that:

infants preferred looking at the more complex pattern

infants could differentiate between two patterns.

Working in pairs, decide why Fantz could draw these two conclusions from his results. Write your explanations down. Each pair then takes it in turn to read out their explanations to the other pairs. Each pair must then discuss in private which of the others has given the most accurate and concise explanations. Take a vote to find the best explanation.

Depth perception

To be able to perceive depth, the infant must be able to perceive that some things are further away than others. This occurs when you look down a flight of stairs or over a cliff: you can tell that the ground drops away. E. Gibson and R. Walk (1960) used the visual cliff apparatus in **laboratory experiments** to test **depth perception**. The equipment consists of a check-patterned surface board which is covered by a large sheet of glass. The patterned surface is immediately under the glass on one side (the 'shallow' side). On the *other* side of the glass the patterned surface is one metre lower (the 'deep drop'), as you can see in Figure 10.6.

Newborn infants cannot move about by themselves; however, six-month-old babies moved over the shallow side towards their mothers but not over the deep side. Gibson and Walk concluded that this suggested depth perception was **innate**.

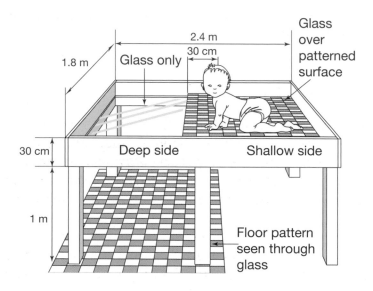

Figure 10.6 Gibson and Walk's visual cliff apparatus

Evaluation of infant studies

Some general criticims of neonate studies are identified at the beginning of this section (p.130). In addition, critics of Gibson and Walk's research argue that as the babies were several months old they might have already **learned** that an abrupt change in the pattern size indicates that the ground 'drops away'. If this is so, depth perception may be learned, which is the **nurture** argument.

Another explanation for this (from the **nature** side) is that depth perception is **innate** but it does not develop until the child is several months old. In research to clarify these points, J. Campos and colleagues (1970) attached heart-rate monitors to babies of various ages when they were on the visual cliff. Results showed that heart rate changed, depending on the age of the baby, as shown in Table 10.1.

From these results it seems that depth perception is apparent by about two months of age, so it is likely to be innate. However, the *implications* of depth may have been learned because such understanding does not develop until nine months of age.

Age of baby	Change in heart rate	Conclusions
Under 2 months	None	No perception of depth
2–9 months	Slows	Interest, so depth perception
9 months +	Increases	Fear, so implications of depth perception

Table 10.1 Relationship between age and change of heart rate in babies on the deep side of visual cliff apparatus

Visual deprivation studies

Some researchers have studied how visual abilities develop when there is no visual stimulation from the environment. Obviously they could not rear human infants in utter darkness as this would be completely **unethical**, but adults who have gained their sight for the first time can provide valuable information. Another advantage is that researchers and participants can talk to each other, so the information gained is very rich.

If newly-sighted people are unable to make sense of what they see, this suggests that perceptual abilities are **learned** through experience. On the other hand, if they can correctly interpret what they see, this suggests that perceptual abilities are largely **innate**.

M. von Senden (1932) summarised the data from 65 people who had gained sight after cataract operations; this data went back over 100 years. He found that:

- **They showed the same abilities as sighted newborns**, such as the ability to separate form from background, fixate objects and follow a moving object.
- **They were unable to recognise** simple objects or shapes which they knew by touch. Some people **learned** to do this, suggesting that exposure to and interaction with the visual environment is necessary for the development of perception. However, it required effort – those who gave up did not learn to make sense of what they saw.
- **They were unable to use sight to make judgements,** such as which of two sticks was the longer: they had to feel the sticks before they could answer.
- **They did not show perceptual constancies**, such as shape constancy (see p.126). So although they could correctly name an object when it was in one position, they could not recognise it in another position.

The evidence above suggests that some perceptual abilities are innate (**nature**) but that experience (**nurture**) is crucial for their development. A **case study** reported by R. Gregory and J. Wallace (1963) adds to this evidence. The man involved was known as S.B. (see Confidentiality, p.188). He was 52 years old when he gained his sight after an operation, and he too showed the kind of abilities and limitations described above. He was too frightened to cross a busy street on his own (which requires **depth perception**) even though he did this confidently when he was blind.

Evaluation of visual deprivation studies

Psychologists must be cautious in drawing conclusions from this kind of research because the adult's visual system is not the same as that of the infant: it may have deteriorated from lack of use and not because of a lack of visual stimulation. In addition, newly-sighted adults have spent years using other senses to compensate for lack of sight, and their dependence on the other senses may hamper their ability to use their new visual information. As an example, S.B. preferred to spend his evenings in the dark, even when he could see. Finally, of course, we cannot generalise from **case studies**.

The role of nurture

Now we turn to ways of studying the role of nurture in the development of perceptual abilities. Some researchers have compared the perception of people from a variety of cultures and others have investigated whether perceptual abilities are adaptable, which would suggest that they are **learned**.

Cross-cultural studies of perception

If people from different environments show differences in perceptual abilties, it suggests that these abilities are due to their environment (**nurture**). **Cross-cultural** research enables psychologists to study this.

W. Hudson (1960) investigated three-dimensional **depth perception** with various tribal groups in Africa using the picture shown in Figure 10.7. The picture includes two of the cues illustrated earlier (see p.128). The cues in the picture (relative size and height in the visual field) help the viewer to perceive depth in the picture. Results showed that members of African tribes were unable to understand this picture. For example, they thought the man was about to spear the elephant. Researchers concluded that they did not have three-dimensional depth perception.

Figure 10.7 A picture to test depth perception

Figure 10.8 This illustration shows that we learn depth cues from an early age

GROUP ACTIVITY – Identifying depth cues

Working alone, see how many monocular depth cues you can identify in Figure 10.8. Why do you think the rocks in the background are hazy? Compare your answers with others in the group.

Evaluation of cross-cultural studies of perception

R. Gross (1999) has summarised criticisms of this research, which centre on the assumptions that Hudson was making. He assumed that these Western conventions for showing depth were in fact universal conventions (an example of **ethnocentrism**). We learn these depth cues from an early age. Figure 10.8 provides an example. Gross adds that later researchers amended Hudson's test picture by adding *other* depth cues – the monocular cues of texture gradient and distance haze – as in Figure 10.9. When these cues were added there was a marked increase in participants' ability to interpret the picture correctly.

Figure 10.9 Hudson's test picture with additional depth cues

Hudson's research underlines a difficulty of **cross-cultural research**, because we are bound in the conventions of our own culture. Researchers thought they were testing depth perception, whereas they were actually testing cultural conventions of how to represent depth in two dimensions. This is not to say that cross-cultural studies have no value, but that psychologists should be aware of their limitations and try to compensate for them.

Perceptual readjustment studies

If perception can be altered, and human beings can adapt to this alteration, this suggests that perception is mostly **learned**. In an effort to demonstrate this, G. Stratton (1896) developed a lens which made his visual world appear upside down and left to right. He wore this over one eye for much of the day for eight days, keeping his other eye covered. When he was not wearing the lens he wore a blindfold. He gradually learned to adjust to his 'upside-down' world – imagine drinking a cup of coffee wearing this lens! He reported seeing the fire in one place, but the sound of the fire crackling came from a different point, so other **cues** from his environment could have helped him make sense of it.

For eight days he never saw his world the right way up, and he got used to moving around in an upside-down world so that he too felt upside-down. He reported that when he removed the lens he soon saw things as 'normal', that is, they did not appear to be odd in comparison with his previous perception of them. It seems that his perception did not change completely; he was probably able to function because he **learned** to adjust his movements. Because Stratton's perceptual system was able to adapt to some extent, this suggests that perception is not completely **innate**, because if it was **innate** then it would be unable to adapt.

A more recent study by I. Kohler (1962) related to colour. He wore lenses which were half green and half red. He found that soon after putting them on he had adapted and colours seemed 'normal'. When he took them off again, though, he saw red where the lens had been green, and green where it had been red – his brain had been compensating for the colours. These results show that Kohler's perception did change, thus supporting the **nurture** view, which is that perception is mostly **learned**.

Evaluation of perceptual readjustment studies

Studies such as these clearly suggest that perception is innate because it cannot be changed. However, they also show how experience can help us adjust to changes, indicating a role for nurture. As the research has been done only with adults, we cannot be sure whether the same abilities are present at birth (nature), develop soon after birth as the infant matures (nature) or develop as the infant interacts with its environment (nurture).

Why is the nature/nurture debate inconclusive?

Research on perceptual abilities has contributed to both sides of the nature/nurture debate, and we have seen that some abilities appear to be innate and others learned. Perceptual abilities which develop after a period of time may be due to **environmental** factors or to **maturational** factors. There are several reasons why it is difficult to investigate which of these is more likely. As we have looked at research we have noted **methodological** problems, such as in studying infants or conducting cross-cultural research.

In addition, there are **ethical** concerns which reduce the researcher's ability to exert control over research, such as:

- In order to separate out innate and learned factors, psychologists would need to deprive infants of any visual experiences over a period of time (perhaps by keeping them blindfolded), and then compare their perceptual abilities with infants reared normally. Obviously this is unthinkable.
- Psychologists cannot deny or offer adults their sight in order to do research. This is why they have experimented on themselves or have studied newly-sighted people. Because these are people who are undergoing traumatic experiences, ethical concern about their physical and psychological wellbeing constrains what psychologists can ask of and do to them.

Because of the methodological and ethical difficulties involved in researching this topic, the results of perceptual development research have so far produced no clear answers. Findings sometimes provide some evidence for both explanations or may even be contradictory. Will new research provide any clear answers? It appears unlikely, because evidence suggests that both nature (innate abilities) and nurture (experience) have a role to play. As a result, researchers have now moved towards an interactionist position – the study of *how* nature and nurture interact – rather than establish which is primarily responsible for the development of perceptual abilities.

The OCR exam

The OCR exam will test your ability to:

- show knowledge and understanding of visual constancies, depth cues and illusions
- consider the role of nature in the development of perceptual abilities, e.g. infant (neonate) studies, deprivation studies
- consider the role of nurture in the development of perceptual abilities, e.g. cross-cultural studies, readjustment studies
- evaluate the research on the development of perceptual abilities in the light of the nature/nurture debate.

Sample exam questions on perception

1. Describe an example of a visual constancy from everyday life. (2 marks)

2. Identify and briefly explain two depth cues. (2+2 marks)

3. a Identify two examples of a visual illusion. (1+1 mark)
   b Explain one of them. (2 marks)

4. a Describe one study of infant perception. (4 marks)
   b Identify one limitation of this study. (2 marks)

5. Describe what is meant by a cross-cultural study in psychological research. (2 marks)

6. Explain what is meant by the nature/nurture debate in psychology. (2 marks)

Bio-psychology

Bio-psychology is concerned with the role that physiology plays in psychological processes and behaviour. This is illustrated in the next two chapters.

Chapter 11 considers Stress, the changes which occur in the body and some possible causes of stress. Chapter 12 concerns Sex and Gender, looking at both biological and psychological aspects.

Stress

Most of us have experienced stress – if you are stuck in a traffic jam, have family problems or have a lot to do and not enough time. Sometimes a series of small setbacks leads us to feel stressed. We feel this stress physically (for instance, increased heart rate or sweating) and psychologically (such as confused thinking or frustration). We will look at these signs of stress in more detail shortly, but first let us consider what stress is.

Defining stress

A widely used definition of stress is the one provided by R. Lazarus and S. Folkman (1984). They define **stress** as:

- 'a pattern of negative physiological states and psychological responses occurring in situations where people perceive threats to their wellbeing which they may be unable to meet.'

This definition suggests that:

- There is an event or situation which causes stress (called the **stressor**), such as unemployment, excessive noise or sitting exams.
- The individual must perceive the event or situation as a threat if it is to cause stress. When we feel unable to cope with the demands of this event or situation, then we see it as a threat.
- A set of physiological and psychological changes take place which can be taken as signs of stress.

Signs of stress

The definition of stress given above refers to both physiological and psychological changes as signs of stress, so we start by considering the physiological (or biological) work of Hans Selye before moving on to psychological signs, which come under the two headings of cognitive and behavioural signs of stress.

Physiological signs – the general adaptation syndrome

In 1936 Hans Selye reported that animals responded in the same way to a variety of damaging experiences such as infection, fear, electric shocks or heat. Later he studied humans and found, for example, that hospital patients showed similar patterns of response. Selye (1976) called this response the General Adaptation Syndrome (GAS). The GAS is defined as a non-specific physiological response that occurs to a variety of stressful stimuli. A key point here is that the response is very similar regardless of the cause. The GAS consists of three phases.

Phase 1 – alarm reaction

When the individual perceives something as a stressor, the alarm reaction is triggered. There is a drop in blood pressure and muscle tension and the body prepares for 'fight or flight'. The main physiological changes are:

- Breathing rate is increased to bring more oxygen to the muscles.
- Heart rate and blood pressure are increased to move blood around the body faster.
- Glucose is released from the liver to provide extra energy.
- Muscles are tensed in preparation for a response such as fighting or running away.
- Sweating occurs to cool the body and allow more energy to be burned.
- Blood is drained from the face and digestion slows down as more blood is made available for the muscles and the brain.

When the threat has gone, the body slowly returns to normal.

Phase 2 – resistance

If the stressor continues, however, the body produces chemicals to bring itself back to normal levels. At the same time, the chemicals produced in Phase 1 continue to be produced but their action uses up some of the body's resources, so the body may be coping with the stressor but its resistance to disease is lowered.

Phase 3 – exhaustion

If the stressor continues, or recurs before the body has been able to recover, resources become exhausted. The body starts to show the effects of prolonged resistance to the stressor; for example:

- kidney damage
- low hormone stores
- low blood sugar
- reduced resistance to infection
- increased activity in the immune system, so that it attacks healthy cells
- illness such as flu, ulcers or heart disease.

Selye's identification of these responses provides a valuable insight into causes of stress-related illness, but he failed to consider why someone may perceive an event as threatening in the first place. Sometimes an event which one person sees as a threat may appear to someone else in a positive way – as a challenge. Helping people to perceive things in a positive way can help them cope with the demands they face and so reduce the effects of stress.

Psychological signs of stress

Cognitive signs of stress include:

- **Confusion or distracted thinking** – people experiencing stress often have difficulties with concentration, memory or logical thought.
- **Emotions** – such as frustration, anger or anxiety (anxiety is a rather general term covering worry, doubts, fears, apprehension or tension).
- **Low levels of mental activity**, very little interest or motivation – this may be a symptom of the helplessness or depression which may develop in someone who is experiencing continued stress.

Our **behaviour** may also be affected by stress in some of the following ways:

- **Physical difficulties** when performing movements, due partly to reduced ability to control the body, trembling or shaking.
- **Restlessness and fidgeting** with clothes, objects, hair and so on.
- **Aggression**, which is sometimes created in a **laboratory experiment** as a way of measuring stress.
- **Slow movements** which may be performed without motivation, or even considerable periods of complete inactivity; these may be symptoms of helplessness or depression in someone experiencing continued stress.

GROUP ACTIVITY – Signs of stress

Divide the group in half. One half will be observers, the other half will imagine how it feels to experience stressors. Below are three situations for you to consider. Choose the column which applies to your role (as observer or as experiencer) and list the possible signs of stress. Remember to consider physiological, cognitive and behavioural signs.

Observing the behaviour of:

candidates whilst they are sitting an exam

someone coming through customs who is about to have their luggage searched

passengers on a very crowded train which is hot and has broken down.

How would you feel if you were:

sitting an exam

waiting to have your luggage searched when you have nothing illegal

a passenger on a hot, crowded train which has broken down.

When you have finished, join the others in your half and compile a master list of the signs you have identified. Then bring both halves of the group together and compare your lists. Discuss how effective the observer could be in identifying signs of stress. Consider, for example, whether the observers have identified behaviour which may not be due to stress? Did the experiencers experience things which the observers could not see? Did they behave in ways which indicate stress but these were not picked up by the observer?

Ways of measuring stress

The final section of this chapter looks at research on causes of stress, so researchers have to measure stress if they want to investigate it, but this can be quite difficult if they want to go beyond physiological measures. We will now examine some of the methods they have used, along with an evaluation of their usefulness.

Physiological ways of measuring stress

Some physiological (biological) changes described above under Selye's Phase 1 can be measured (see Figure 11.1) and thus provide objective indicators of levels of stress, such as increase in:

- **Breathing rate** – can be measured through tubes which are placed around the chest.
- **Blood pressure** – can be measured using a specially designed inflated armband.
- **Heart rate** – can be measured using an electrocardiogram (ECG).

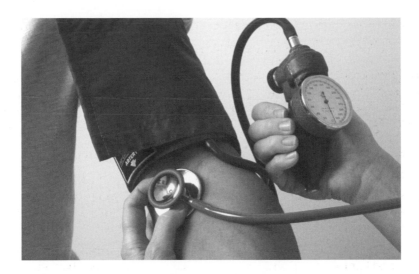

Figure 11.1 This woman's blood pressure is being measured

- **Sweating** – can be measured using the galvanic skin response (GSR): electrodes sensitive to the salts in sweat are attached to the palm of the hand and the current is measured by a voltage meter.
- **Levels of hormones and steroids** in the blood or urine – can be measured using chemical tests on blood or urine samples.

Evaluation of physiological measures of stress

The major advantage of these physiological measures is that they provide objective indicators of stress. However, they also present several difficulties which may lead to inaccurate results and conclusions. Difficulties include:

- The nature of these measures, such as being wired up to a machine or having to give a urine sample, may create additional stress. This will increase stress levels even further, but the researcher will not know how much of the stress is due to the original stressor and how much is due to the process of measurement.
- If a participant is taking part in an **experiment**, being 'wired up' like this suggests that the experiment is related to their physiological state. This is an example of a **demand characteristic** (see p.180), and it may affect the results of the experiment.
- Physiological measures can be used in a **laboratory experiment** but are very difficult to use in a less formal setting.

Despite these difficulties, physiological measures can provide some data for research. However, a much fuller picture is gained if they are combined with psychological measures of stress, as you will see now.

Psychological ways of measuring stress

These measures include **surveys** – both **questionnaires** and **interviews** – which are subjective measures because people are asked about themselves. In contrast, behavioural measures are taken by other people and provide more objective (but not necessarily more accurate) information. Each method has drawbacks.

Surveys

Details of how to prepare surveys, and their strengths and weaknesses, are given on p.176. Questions must be clear and unambiguous, and must not persuade the participant to answer in a particular way, as this would bias the answers.

Examples of the way the two types of survey may be used in stress are:

● **Questionnaires** can provide a lot of information cheaply, which is easy to quantify and may benefit both the researcher and the respondent (see p.176 for more details). The example in Figure 11.2 was designed to help athletes to be aware of stress and to monitor their stress responses just before competing. You can see that it includes both **physiological** and **psychological** elements.
● **Interviews** enable the researcher to probe more deeply into the participant's experiences with open-ended questions such as 'Describe how your body feels at the moment?' or 'How do you cope when you have to do several things at once?'.

Evaluation of surveys

Interviews provide rich information but it may be specific to the individual or the situation; such information cannot be **generalised** to the population as a whole. The researcher may have to interpret the answers in order to compare them with answers from other people, which may distort the results (see p.177 for more details).

When responding to questionnaires or interviews, people may give socially desirable answers, they may lie, exaggerate or answer carelessly due to boredom. Any of these factors may distort the results.

If respondents guess that questions about their work or their family relationships are designed to measure stress, this may affect their responses: they might exaggerate the level of stress they experience because many other people report work-related stress and they want to be helpful to the researcher. In other words, cues from the questions have created **demand characteristics** (see p.180).

Directions: a number of statements which athletes have used to describe their feelings before competition are given below. Read each statement and then circle the appropriate number to the right of the statement to indicate how you feel right now – at this moment. There are no right or wrong answers. Do not spend too much time on any one statement, but choose the answer which describes your feelings right now.

	Not at all	Somewhat	Moderately so	Very much so
1 I am concerned about this competition	1	2	3	4
2 I feel nervous	1	2	3	4
3 I feel at ease	1	2	3	4
4 I have self-doubts	1	2	3	4
5 I feel jittery	1	2	3	4
6 I feel comfortable	1	2	3	4
7 I am concerned that I may not do as well in this competition as I could	1	2	3	4
8 My body feels tense	1	2	3	4
9 I feel self-confident	1	2	3	4
10 I am concerned about losing	1	2	3	4
11 I feel tense in my stomach	1	2	3	4
12 I feel secure	1	2	3	4
13 I am concerned about choking under pressure	1	2	3	4
14 My body feels relaxed	1	2	3	4
15 I'm confident I can meet the challenge	1	2	3	4
16 I am concerned about performing poorly	1	2	3	4
17 My heart is racing	1	2	3	4
18 I'm confident about performing well	1	2	3	4

Figure 11.2 An extract from the Competitive State Anxiety Inventory 2

Laboratory experiments

In the more controlled environment of a laboratory experiment, several ways of measuring stress have been devised which are more objective than the survey methods we have considered. These measures include:

- **Accuracy** on a task in a stressful and non-stressful condition.
- **Time taken** to complete a task in a stressful and non-stressful condition.
- **Level of electric shocks** participants give to a confederate, as a measure of frustration or aggression.

Evaluation of laboratory experiments

Although there is a gain in objective measurement of stress, the artificial nature of the laboratory experiment may create **demand characteristics** and thus increase a participant's stress level simply because they know they are being studied. In addition, participants may not give shocks for moral reasons, however stressed they feel. These factors would bias the results.

Another disadvantage is that artificially created situations of stress can only measure the immediate consequences for the individual. It is very difficult to measure other, longer term effects if they occur outside the laboratory setting. In addition, people may show physiological evidence of stress yet not feel it: for example, heart rate and blood pressure may increase in someone experiencing a noisy environment, yet when asked they do not report feeling stress. People rarely classify noise as a source of stress unless specifically asked.

Finally, there are ethical concerns about creating stress, frustration and aggression in other people, about allowing participants to use what appear to be electric shocks on another person, and about following up participants to ensure there are no long-term effects for them.

Research into possible causes of stress

We have just considered some of the ways of measuring stress and the difficulties associated with these research methods. Keep these points in mind as you read the next section, which describes some research on the possible causes of stress.

Heat

Reviews of statistics on violence (such as riots and domestic violence) in the USA showed that violence levels increased as temperatures reached about 30°C. This **correlation** could have been caused because more alcohol is drunk in hot weather or because people meet together out of doors more. However, these possible causes do not explain a further finding, which is that at temperatures above 30°C violence levels *decrease*.

R. Baron and P. Bell (1975) tested this in a **laboratory experiment**, measuring aggression as an indicator of stress by noting the level of electric shocks a participant gave to a confederate. Results showed that heat caused increases in aggression in participants who were not angry and reduced aggression levels in those who were angry. One possible explanation is that the participants who were made angry experienced discomfort which was made worse by the heat. In order to reduce the high levels of discomfort they refrained from being aggressive.

Architecture

The design of buildings can increase stress. This may occur in open-plan offices, badly lit rooms or poorly designed buildings. A field study by S. Valins and A. Baum (1973) compared a high-density design of student accommodation with one of low density, as described in Table 11.1.

Density	Type of accommodation	Description	Amount of contact with others
High density	Corridor design	17 double bedrooms, all sharing one bathroom and one lounge	Frequent contact with many others and limited use of facilities
Low density	Suite design	Two or three bedrooms grouped with one bathroom and one lounge	Limited contact with others and easy access to facilities

Table 11.1 Description of high- and low-density student accommodation

Both designs provided the same amount of space per person and required two to share a bedroom, but a **survey** of students living in the building which created high-density living showed they were less sociable, having more unwanted social contact and feeling more crowded.

Noise

Noise is sometimes defined as unwanted sound. **Laboratory experiments** show that noise triggers the reactions associated with stress, particularly when the noise is loud, unpredictable or uncontrollable. When people are able to control noise levels, they are less likely to perceive the noise as a stressor.

A study of noise in the work-place was conducted by E. Cottington and colleagues (1983). They compared several hundred workers in two factories, one of which had a noisier environment than the other. The researchers:

● **interviewed** the workers to find out their health habits, their work and medical histories
● gave out **questionnaires** asking workers about their relationships with others, attitudes to work and job satisfaction
● **measured blood pressure** regularly in the workers.

Results showed that those working in the noisier factory had higher blood pressure and greater dissatisfaction with work, suggesting that they experienced higher levels of stress. However, because this was a **natural experiment** the researchers were not able to control all the variables in the two factories, such as the noise levels, the work practices or management style. Any or all of these could have contributed to the results. For more details on variables see p.179.

TREES AND STRESS

People's physical signs of stress, such as muscle tension and pulse rate, are measurably reduced within as little as three to four minutes after moving into leafy surroundings, researchers in the *Journal of Environmental Psychology* claim. Trees can also reduce levels of stress caused by noise pollution, and hospital patients who can see trees recover faster than those who can see only buildings, says a report in *Science*.

Pollution

Research on pollution has shown that people are frequently unaware of it: they only notice it when it is visible, like smog, or when it smells strongly or creates physical discomfort. Pollution (such as carbon monoxide, lead or the mix of chemicals in the air known as 'smog') itself causes similar symptoms to the symptoms of stress. Participants in a polluted environment may therefore show higher blood pressure, increased breathing rate, loss of memory, irritability or illness. Researchers must try to tease apart the stress symptoms due to the pollution itself and those related to awareness of pollution.

Overall, research suggests that pollution may add to stress in individuals who are already stressed. G. Evans and colleagues (1987) **surveyed** 500 residents of Los Angeles over three years. They noted the participants' *perception* of pollution levels, not the actual level of pollution. They also asked them questions relating to their emotional state and stressful life events (such as those on the Holmes–Rahe scale, see p.154). People who perceived pollution to be moderate were those who were more highly stressed. Those reporting no stressful life events perceived pollution as being at a lower level.

Crowding

Being crowded with other people can cause stress, which U. Lundberg (1976) claimed was due to arousal. He monitored arousal levels of male passengers on a commuter train and results showed that passengers who boarded at the beginning of the journey (when it was fairly empty) experienced less arousal than those who joined later when the train became more crowded.

Figure 11.3 Road rage may be the result of several stressors – this man will show the physiological responses identified by Selye under phase 1

Although both groups experienced a crowded environment, those boarding the train earlier would have been able to choose where they sat and so have more control over their **personal space**. Those joining later had to invade the personal space of others, they had fewer options as to where and how they positioned themselves and this made them feel less in control. For more on Personal space see p.16.

Stressful life events

We have seen that stress can be a cause of illness, and T. Holmes and R. Rahe (1967) devised a way of measuring stress in order to predict the likelihood of illness. By surveying the life changes of 5,000 patients they identified 43 life-change events. People were then asked to give a value to each event in terms of the amount of social adjustment the average person would need to make to cope with the change. The events were then ranked in order of value to form the Social Readjustment Rating Scale (SRRS) as shown in Figure 11.4.

Rank	Life event	Mean value
1	Death of spouse	100
2	Divorce	73
3	Marital separation	65
4	Jail term	63
5	Death of close family member	63
6	Personal injury or illness	53
7	Marriage	50
8	Fired at work	47
9	Marital reconciliation	45
10	Retirement	45
11	Change in health of family member	44
12	Pregnancy	40
13	Sex difficulties	39
14	Gain of new family member	39
15	Business readjustment	39
16	Change in financial state	38
17	Death of close friend	37
18	Change to different line of work	36
19	Change in number of arguments with spouse	35
20	Mortgage over $10,000	31
21	Foreclosure of mortgage or loan	30
22	Change in responsibilities at work	29
23	Son or daughter leaving home	29
24	Trouble with in-laws	29
25	Outstanding personal achievement	28
26	Wife begins or stops work	26
27	Begin or end school	26
28	Change in living conditions	25
29	Revision of personal habits	24
30	Trouble with boss	23
31	Change in work hours or conditions	20
32	Change in residence	20
33	Change in schools	20
34	Change in recreation	19
35	Change in church activities	19
36	Change in social activities	18
37	Mortgage or loan less than $10,000	17
38	Change in sleeping habits	16
39	Change in number of family get-togethers	15
40	Change in eating habits	15
41	Vacation	13
42	Christmas	12
43	Minor violations of the law	11

Figure 11.4 Holmes and Rahe's Social Readjustment Rating Scale

GROUP ACTIVITY – Devising your own social readjustment rating scale

Devise your own Social Readjustment Rating Scale by following these steps.

1 Look through the SRRS (Figure 11.4) and add any life events you think are important but have been omitted.
2 From this new list choose the 30 life events which you feel require the most social adjustment, and write these clearly on a piece of paper (for use in step 4).
3 On another piece of paper rank these events from 1–30: the life event requiring the most adjustment will be ranked as No.1. When you have completed this ranking, you will have created your own Social Readjustment Rating Scale. Keep it for step 6.
4 Take the paper with your list of 30 life events (created in step 2) and exchange it with a partner.
5 Look at your partner's list and rank their list of life events from 1–30. Return this list to your partner. Your partner also ranks your 30 life events and returns your list.
6 Compare how your partner has ranked your 30 life events with your own ranking of them in your SRRS. Discuss any differences in your evaluations. Would you change your mind as a result of your partner's ideas?

The assumption is that changes in your life create demands. The more difficulty you have in coping with these demands, the greater the stress. In addition, if you have several such changes in a short period of time, stress is even greater and, according to Selye's explanation (see p.144), illness will be more likely.

Evaluation of the SRRS

Some investigators using this scale have found a relationship between high levels of life change and psychological or physical illness. However, others have not, and the scale has been criticised because it does not differentiate between positive and negative changes, which may affect stress levels differently (one person may be dreading retirement but another looking forward to it).

Another criticism is that some stressful life events are not included – you might be able to think of some. Because Holmes and Rahe were interested in 'normal' life events, they did not include events such as the unexpected catastrophe – a plane crash or nuclear accident – and natural disasters such as an earthquake or flooding. For instance, on the day of the Los Angeles earthquake in 1994 there were five times as many deaths from sudden heart attacks. Researchers J. Muller and R. Verrier (1996) reported that only 13 per cent of these were due to physical exertion (such as running or lifting debris) and that stress was a likely trigger for the others.

Research also shows increases in stress-related illnesses in people who have experienced or helped in such catastrophes. This is known as toxic stress, and may last for months or even years.

Another point is that stress is also generated by the small, everyday hassles of living such as having too much to do, managing money, social obligations, and these are stressors which are not included in the SRRS. A. Kanner and colleagues (1981) compared the impact of hassles, as opposed to major life events, on health. Their research found that the higher a person's rating on the hassles scale, the poorer their physical and psychological health. In contrast, when everyday positive experiences, called 'uplifts' are measured, these are associated with physical and psychological wellbeing.

The OCR exam

The OCR exam will test your ability to:

- define stress, e.g. Selye's GAS model
- demonstrate knowledge of the physiological (biological) and psychological (cognitive and behavioural) signs of stress
- describe physiological and psychological ways of measuring stress
- demonstrate knowledge of research into possible causes of stress, e.g. heat, noise, pollution, architecture, crowding, stressful life events.

Sample exam questions on stress

1. Explain what is meant by the term 'stress'. (2 marks)
2. Identify two psychological signs of stress. (1+1 mark)
3. a Describe one physiological (biological) way of measuring stress. (2 marks)
   b Suggest one problem with measuring stress in this way. (2 marks)
4. a Describe what is meant by a survey in psychological research. (2 marks)
   b Identify one limitation of the survey method. (2 marks)
5. a Outline one study that has been carried out to investigate stress; for example, heat, noise etc. (4 marks)
   b Give one criticism of the research you have outlined above. (2 marks)
6. Identify two life events which are thought to cause stress. (1+1 mark)
7. Explain what is meant by debriefing in psychological research. (2 marks)

Sex and Gender

'Is it a girl or a boy?' is one of the first questions a new parent asks. The answer will affect how the baby is treated and how the child views itself. Our society has different expectations of men and women, and the growing child soon learns what they are. But to what extent are these differences due to our biological make-up? This chapter first considers biological differences between males and females and then reviews several explanations for how children come to adopt the attitudes and behaviours which their society considers appropriate to their sex. The chapter ends by looking at the way a variety of cultures view the role of males and females in their society.

Definitions of sex and gender

The words sex and gender are sometimes used as though they mean the same thing, and on other occasions as though they have different meanings. They do have different meanings, as you can see:

- **Sex** refers to biological aspects of the individual. For example, a child's sex is identified at birth by its genitals.
- **Gender** refers to the psychological and cultural aspects of maleness or femaleness.

Psychologists use these two words when they are discussing topics such as how our sense of being male, or of being female, develops. As we will also use them in this chapter, the following definitions will help you understand what these terms mean:

- **Sex identity** – the biological status of being male or female.
- **Gender identity** – some adults whose sex identity is male say they feel as though they are female, so we say their gender identity is female. Gender identity therefore refers to a person's concept of themselves as either masculine or feminine.

- **Sex typing (or gender typing)** – treating people in accordance with society's expectations of them because of their sex: for example, giving mechanical toys to boys and make-up sets to girls.
- **Androgyny** – the set of behaviours which includes high levels of both masculine and feminine characteristics. This term was used by S. Bem (1975) as a result of her work on masculinity and femininity, which she published in a book called *Fluffy Women and Chesty Men*.
- **Gender role** – the set of expectations that society has about what behaviours, characteristics, attitudes, jobs and so on are appropriate for males and for females, what they are 'supposed' to do or be.

GROUP ACTIVITY – Is biology destiny? (Part 1)

This is an extract from *Psychology: A New Introduction* by R. Gross *et al.* (2000), which describes the ideas of G. Wilson (1994). When you have read through it answer the questions.

'Wilson states that the reason 95 per cent of bank managers, company directors, judges and university professors in Britain are men is that men are "more competitive", and because "dominance is a personality characteristic determined by male hormones". Women who do achieve promotion to top management positions "may have brains that are masculinised". Even if women are considered to have the abilities to perform well in professional jobs, they have personality defects (in particular low self-esteem and lack of assertiveness) which impede performance. According to Wilson: "These differences (in mental abilities, motivation, personality and values) are deep-rooted, based in biology, and not easily dismantled by social engineering. Because of them we are unlikely to see the day when the occupational profiles of men and women are the same."'

1. Give two examples of biological differences between men and women, according to Wilson.
2. What qualities does Wilson expect males to have?

Compare your answers with a partner's. Later in this chapter (on p.161) there are some more questions about this extract.

Biological factors in sex differences

Biologically there are a number of ways in which males and females differ, and these are described below:

- **Genetics** – the major determinant of sex is the pairing of chromosomes, each of which is composed of hundreds of genes. Genetically, females have two X chromosomes, making an XX pair; males have an XY pairing.

- **Gonads** – the reproductive organs: in females these are the ovaries and in males the testes. Genes on the Y chromosome cause the reproductive organs in the embryo to develop into testes. Without the action of these genes the organs will develop into ovaries. When the gonads have developed in the foetus, genetic influence stops and hormones take over biological sexual development.
- **Hormones** – the chemicals that affect the development of the internal reproductive structures and the external organs (the genitals). The testes in the male foetus produce testosterone which leads to the development of the penis and scrotum. The ovaries in the female foetus produce oestrogen and progesterone which lead to the development of the womb and the vagina. In fact, both sexes produce these hormones, but in different quantities.

For most individuals all the above features correspond; for example, a boy will have XY chromosome pairing, testes, higher levels of testosterone, a penis and scrotum. However, sometimes development does not follow this pattern and a baby may have an XX chromosome pairing (female), yet have male genitals.

One example of an unusual pattern of development was found in the Batista family in the Dominican Republic. Four of the children who were born with normal female genitals were reared as girls. However, at about 12 years of age they started to develop male genitals and other male features, so that as adults they appeared to be male.

The hormone which creates external male features was absent in the foetus, so the infant appeared to be female at birth. When the child reached puberty, this hormone was produced in sufficient quantities to trigger the external changes which should have occurred before birth. The researchers, J. Imperato-McGinley and colleagues (1974), noted that several other families in the Batista's village were affected like this. All had a common ancestor, which confirmed the likelihood that this unusual development was due to a genetic irregularity.

As we have seen, the genitals are the usual indicators of the sex of the newborn infant because they are visible, and it is from this point that the child's development is influenced by its experiences. Below we examine three explanations for how the developing child comes to adopt the behaviours and attitudes which society sees as appropriate to its sex – in other words, its **gender role** development.

Social learning theory and gender roles

According to social learning theory a girl learns how to be a girl, and a boy how to be a boy, through the major processes of social learning. Details of these processes, which are based on the work of Albert Bandura, are described on p.42. Here we will examine how they explain gender role development.

Observation

Children notice what other people do and how they do it, what they say and how they say it. They notice how other people respond to what is said or done, so they observe the consequences of other people's behaviour. As a result of this observation, the child may then imitate, or copy, the behaviour.

Models

Anyone whose behaviour is observed like this is called a model. The type of people who are more likely to be models are those who are:

- **Similar** – so the child is more likely to observe the behaviour of someone who is the same sex. They also learn what is appropriate for their sex by noting how often a behaviour is performed by others of the same sex. This indicates to them what is typical of their own sex, as well as of the other sex.
- **Powerful or caring** – such as a parent or teacher. The parent of the same sex is a very influential model, according to social learning theory.
- **Reinforced** – if the child sees that the model's behaviour leads to pleasant consequences (such as gaining approval), it is called **vicarious reinforcement** because the child is reinforced indirectly. So a boy who sees a man congratulated for his bravery is more likely to act bravely himself than if the model had not been congratulated; a girl who hears a young woman being told how pretty she looks will be more likely to copy the young woman's appearance.

Imitation

The child may later imitate the model's behaviour, which may be one reason why children enjoy **gender-typed** toys and activities. For instance, girls like make-up because they see women using it, while boys prefer playing football because that is what men do. Adults often support this by providing toys which enable children to imitate the behaviour of same-sex models.

Reinforcement and punishment

The child is more likely to perform the behaviour if they are **reinforced** for doing so. Adults often reward children for behaving in accordance with their gender role. So a boy who continues playing football when he is hurt will be congratulated for being brave, a girl who plays at feeding her dolls may be told what a good mother she is.

Figure 12.1 These toys encourage the child to adopt sex-typed behaviour

Children's peers also provide **reinforcement** and **punishment** – boys make fun of other boys when they do not conform to 'boy' behaviour (for instance, when a boy cries or dresses up in girl's clothes). However, his mother may respond differently, agreeing that he looks pretty. This is how the child learns when it is appropriate to behave in particular ways. Because dressing in girl's clothes brings **punishment** (ridicule), he is less likely to do it in front of his friends. However, he may continue to dress up when Mum is around, because her positive response provides **reinforcement**.

GROUP ACTIVITY – Is biology destiny? (Part 2)

Look again at the extract in the group activity on p.158. Working in pairs, try to answer the following questions together:

1 What do you think Wilson means by 'social engineering'?
2 Using the principles of social learning theory, explain why 95 per cent of bank managers, company directors, judges and university professors in Britain are men.

Compare your answers with other pairs. Take a vote to decide which pair has provided the most accurate and concise answer to question 2.

Research shows that fathers tend to encourage gender-typed behaviour more than mothers do. In particular, they show greater concern about their sons, encouraging them to be active and independent but discouraging them from crying or showing weakness. This could be why boys make fun of boys who do not conform: they are imitating the behaviour of their fathers.

Through **imitation** and **reinforcement** the child gradually adopts appropriate gender role behaviours. As a result of their research, K. Bussey and A. Bandura (1984) have proposed that **gender-typed** behaviour is *initially* shaped by the responses of others (for example, reinforcement such as 'What a big strong boy you are') but as the child gets older he constructs his own personal understanding of his gender role.

Evaluation of the social learning theory explanation

This theory proposes that the child's gender role develops gradually as the child's experiences increase. Gender differences occur because society reinforces behaviour which is considered appropriate to the child's sex, while differences in gender role between girls and boys reflect what the child sees in society and which could therefore be changed.

Figure 12.2 Billy Elliott persisted in behaviour he did not see modelled by males

However, some weaknesses in social learning theory are that:

- **Children show gender-typed preferences** for toys and imitation of same-sex models by about two years of age. Reinforcement and modelling are, by themselves, unlikely to produce such strong preferences at such a young age.
- **Children persist in behaviour** which they do not see modelled. The film *Billy Elliott* is an example of this. Billy was drawn to ballet and desperately wanted to be a ballet dancer, despite being surrounded by men who were typical of the male stereotype. The only ballet dancers he saw were female, but he did not want to be female, he was comfortable as a male. He just wanted to dance.
- **Social learning theory** fails to take account of genetics. Parents and others may be reacting to innate differences in the behaviour of boys and girls.

Psychoanalytic theory and gender roles

According to Freud's psychoanalytic theory, instinctive drives underlie human behaviour. The way we cope with one of these drives – the libido, or life instinct – is what underpins the development of our gender role. Freud proposed that:

- **At about four years of age** the child's **libido** creates a desire for the opposite-sex parent. However, the child also fears that the same-sex parent will be very angry when this desire is discovered. This creates anxiety in the child, because of his conflicting emotions of desire and fear, but the child is not aware of these feelings because they are in his **unconscious**.
- **A boy experiences the Oedipus conflict** because of his desire for his mother and fear that his father will castrate him. To resolve this conflict (to reduce anxiety), the boy **identifies** with his father – he adopts his father's behaviours, speech and attitudes. The boy feels that his father is less likely to harm him, and behaving like his father will bring the boy closer to his mother. So the boy internalises male characteristics through **identification** with his father and starts to behave as a male.
- **A girl experiences the Electra conflict:** she has unconscious longings for her father and fears loss of her mother's love. Because she thinks she has already been castrated by her mother, she is not so fearful of her as the boy is of his father. Her **identification** with her mother, in order to reduce the conflict, is therefore less strong than that of the boy with his father. Nevertheless, she adopts the characteristics of her mother and so her gender role develops.

Figure 12.3 This boy has identified with his father and is adopting his behaviours

 Evaluation of the psychoanalytic explanation

Although psychoanalytic theory has had a huge impact on ideas in the wider world as well as in psychology, it is difficult to gain evidence to support or to disprove it. This is in part because Freud's ideas of the libido, ego and repression are difficult to measure, and therefore to test. Another factor is that because our drives and the causes of our anxiety are in the **unconscious**, they are inaccessible for observing or testing.

However, research has produced criticisms of Freud's explanation for gender-role development. As an example, according to this explanation, children raised in one-parent families should have a poorly developed gender role (because they do not have a parent of each sex or there is only a same-sex parent). Research indicates that this is not the case, and that these children develop gender role as successfully as those raised by two parents.

There are also methodological criticisms of Freud's work, which formed the basis for his theory:

- He relied on patients' memories, which may have been poor or inaccurate.
- The theory was based on **case studies** of a few middle-class (mainly female) patients with severe emotional problems, so his sample was not representative of the population.
- He did not study children directly, yet his theories are based on childhood experiences.

He devised his theory after spending many hours listening to his patients: an example of the **case study** method. As we saw above, this method provides a small and biased sample, so conclusions should not be **generalised** to the wider population.

A final criticism reflects the point made under social learning theory, which is that children much younger than four are aware of gender roles, such as preferring gender-typed toys and activities. Try this out for yourself by completing the activity on page 167.

Cognitive development and gender roles

L. Kohlberg (1966) believed that the child's cognitive development was the most important factor in the development of gender role. He proposed that once the child understands that gender does not change, it has achieved **gender identity**. This develops in three stages: if you look at Piaget's theory of cognitive development (p.72) you will see how it underpins Kohlberg's stages.

Stage 1 – gender labelling (up to three years old)

By about 18 months of age the child knows what 'label' it is – boy or girl – and by the age of two-and-a-half years it can 'label' other children and adults. However, the child does not understand that:

- we stay the same sex throughout life, so a little girl may say she will be a daddy when she grows up
- we stay the same even if we change our appearance to resemble someone of the other sex.

Stage 2 – gender stability (three to five years old)

Gender stability is achieved when the child understands that one's sex remains unchanged throughout life; a four-year-old girl will know that she will become a woman when she grows up. Nevertheless, the child is not yet sure about other people's sex because she can be deceived by appearances, saying that a man who puts on a dress would be a lady. Clothes are one of the ways we differentiate between males and females – they are a cultural definition of sex.

Figure 12.4 Children who are at the stage of gender stability are often confused by 'female' pantomime characters

Stage 3 – gender constancy (from six years old onwards)

When a child understands that gender remains constant in other people as well, despite changes in appearance or voice, they have achieved gender constancy. This relates to the idea of **conservation** – the understanding that something remains essentially the same even though its appearance changes (see p.75).

Kohlberg proposed that once the child has this full understanding of gender, it pays more attention to people who are of the same sex as itself, and adopts their behaviours, attitudes and values – the child's gender role develops. This does not happen until it fully understands that gender is unchangeable.

Evaluation of the cognitive-developmental explanation

Two strengths of the cognitive-developmental explanation are, first, that it accounts for the evidence that children brought up in single- or same-sex families do not have difficulties with gender identity, because the family is not a key part of this explanation; and second, it can also explain why, after about six years of age, children pay more attention to those of the same sex and seek out gender-typed activities.

However, its major weakness is that it cannot account for the two-year-old's strong preference for toys, friends and activities which are gender-related, because this is the age when children still think they could grow up to be someone of the other sex.

Nevertheless, as we see in the next section, there is cross-cultural research which supports Kohlberg's stages, suggesting that this development in understanding is based on **innate** rather than **cultural** factors.

GROUP ACTIVITY – When do children know gender roles?

Using old magazines or catalogues, cut out pictures of things which are usually associated more with one sex than the other: for example, clothes, sports equipment, toys, activities. Make sure the pictures are clear, and are of things which the average five-year-old would be familiar with. Paste each picture on a card.

Try to find children between the ages of about three and seven years old and ask their parents if you can show them some pictures and ask them questions. Show the parents the cards and tell them the questions. Then show the child each card in turn and ask them to say whether the picture is related to males or females. Keep the questions simple. For example, you could ask 'Is this toy for a girl or a boy?' or 'Who would wear this – a lady or a man?'.

Make sure you note the child's age and answer to each question. Can you see any patterns in the results? Do older children give more correct answers? At what age could you say that children seem to know which pictures are associated with males and which with females? Which ethical concerns have you taken account of?

Cultural differences in gender role development

Comparison between different cultures is useful because, if the same pattern of characteristics or behaviours occurs, this suggests that it is largely based on **innate** factors. On the other hand, if there are differences between cultures, this suggests that our experiences and the **environment** we grow up in have considerable influence on our development.

An example of the influence of the environment comes from M. Mead's (1935) study of three primitive societies in New Guinea. She noted huge differences in the roles, behaviours and expectations of males and females, namely that:

● The **Arapesh** tribe showed similar behaviours, regardless of sex. Both men and women were gentle and affectionate and shared the rearing of children equally.

- The **Mundugumor** tribe also showed similar behaviours, but here both men and women were aggressive and competitive; children and child-bearing were disliked.
- The **Tchambuli** tribe had distinctive **gender roles**, but the males were dependent and spent much of their time making crafts and grooming themselves, whereas the women supported and managed the family and were more dominant.

Mead concluded that differences between the sexes were culturally, not biologically, created. Nevertheless, she did note that there were some **innate** differences, because in these cultures men did generally tend to be more aggressive than women.

This work is widely quoted as evidence of the importance of culture in gender-role development, but critics argue that Mead exaggerated the differences between the Arapesh and the Mundugumor tribes. She was an anthropologist, not a psychologist, and in her later work she argued that women were naturally more nurturing than men.

R. Munroe and colleagues (1984) compared the understanding of gender across four cultures, in Kenya, Nepal, Belize and Samoa. They found a consistent pattern: that children first come to understand that they will stay the same sex throughout life, but can still be confused about the sex of others when those people change their appearance.

In some cultures, such as the Mojave Indians of North America, there are more than two gender roles. Apart from conventional male and female roles, there are males who choose to live as females and females who choose to live as males.

It is increasingly difficult to find cultures completely isolated from other cultures, and therefore to separate biological from environmental factors. In general, though, **cross-cultural research** shows that the female gender role is more likely to involve childcare whereas the males are more likely to be dominant in the social structure.

The OCR exam

The OCR exam will test your ability to:

- define sex typing, sex identity, gender identity and androgyny (Bem)
- demonstrate knowledge of biological factors in sex differences, e.g. the role of hormones and genetics
- demonstrate knowledge of alternative explanations of sex/gender-role development, e.g. social learning theory, psychoanalytic approach (Freud), cognitive approach (Kohlberg)
- consider cultural differences in gender-role development.

Sample exam questions

1 Explain what is meant by the term 'sex identity'? (2 marks)

2 Identify and briefly explain two factors that cause biological differences between males and females. (2+2 marks)

3 a Describe the psychoanalytic approach (Freud) to gender development. (4 marks)

   b Suggest one criticism that can be made of this approach. (2 marks)

4 Explain what is meant by the term 'imitation' in social learning theory. (2 marks)

5 Kohlberg's cognitive approach of gender-role development suggests three stages of understanding.

   a Identify one of these stages. (1 mark)

   b Describe the child's understanding of gender at this stage. (2 marks)

6 Outline two cultural differences between males and females that have been observed by psychologists. (2+2 marks)

Research in Psychology

Psychologists discover more about human behaviour by using a variety of research methods. These methods are explored in the next two chapters.

Chapter 13 considers various methods, their advantages and disadvantages. Chapter 14 describes how to plan, carry out and write up an investigation, starting with the important topic of ethics.

Research Methods

H ugh Coolican (1995) says there are three major ways in which psychologists obtain information about people – 'you ask them, watch them or meddle'. This chapter describes the ways in which psychologists ask, watch and meddle. In other words, we are going to look at research methods. Some of them permit a high degree of control, others are devised to study how people behave naturally, some generate information which is easy to count (or quantify), whereas others focus more on experience. We also consider how to choose the most appropriate method, variables and ways of measuring behaviour.

Observational method

When psychologists observe, they watch and analyse people's behaviour. It is usual to have more than one observer because behaviour is complex and the observer may be biased. If the behaviour is videoed, the observers will analyse the behaviour from the video. They need to be trained how to analyse and measure the behaviour being studied so that they all interpret it in the same way. This is called **inter-observer reliability**.

Behaviour is noted on an **observation schedule**. The researchers must decide what behaviours are to be noted (see Measuring the dependent variable, p.179), how the participants will be observed and over what time period. Is it better to watch six children for a 15-minute period or two children for a full play-group session or any child who comes to the sand box?

Researchers may run a pilot study because they can watch the kind of behaviour they will be analysing, and thus devise the most useful measures. Figure 13.1 shows a simple schedule for observation of co-operation in children's play: each participant is identified by a number in order to preserve anonymity (see Ethics, p.188).

The observational method can be used for a variety of purposes, as described below.

Naturalistic observation

Here the researchers have no control, they are not participants but look at behaviour which occurs naturally, as it would in a school playground, for example. Before starting the study, the observers try to become familiar to those they are observing, in order to minimise the effect that their presence may have.

- **Advantages** – the behaviour occurs in its natural setting; observation provides very detailed information; it can be used as a starting point for further, more controlled, research; it can be used when other methods might be unethical.
- **Disadvantages** – the presence of observers could influence the behaviour of those being observed; it is difficult for observers to be completely objective; many variables could affect behaviour so that it is not possible to draw any conclusions.

Controlled observation

This type of observation is frequently used with children or in social psychology research. Controlled observations are essentially **laboratory experiments** because an **independent variable** is being tested and control is possible. In order that control can be exerted and so that the behaviour is easier to observe (such as through one-way mirrors) the observations may take place in an artificial setting such as a research laboratory. One example is Bandura's study of aggression (p.44).

| Participant number | Number of times behaviour occurred | | | | |
	gave object	smiled at other	physically assisted other	agreed to help	encouraged other
1					
2					
3					
4					
5					
6					

Figure 13.1 An example of a simple observational schedule for recording measures of co-operative behaviour during children's play

- **Advantages** – by controlling some variables (see p.178), it is possible for the researchers to draw conclusions from their observations.
- **Disadvantages** – the unfamiliar setting may affect participants' behaviour, making it less natural.

Participant observation

Here the observer becomes one of the group of people that he or she wishes to observe. The observer may tell the others that they will be observed (an overt observation), or may pretend to be one of the group and not inform them that they are being observed (a covert observation). This method raises particular **ethical issues**, such as deception, observing people in private, perhaps hearing personal or confidential information, and not gaining people's consent to be part of an investigation.

- **Advantages** – participant observation allows researchers to observe people in a natural setting and gain some understanding of the causes of their behaviour; it is particularly useful for studying the way people behave when they are in groups.
- **Disadvantages** – the observer may be unable to make notes until they are away from the group, there may be difficulties remembering accurately, or the observer may interpret or record information in a biased way; if the others in the group know they are being observed, this may affect their behaviour, making it less natural; ethical guidelines may not be maintained.

Case study

The case study is an in-depth study of one person or a small number of people. It may include **interviews** (using open-ended questions) of the person being studied as well as others who can provide information about the person's past or present experiences and behaviours. Data provided by school or medical records may also be gathered. Case studies are often used for investigating people who show unusual abilities or difficulties: for example, adults who have gained sight for the first time (see Visual deprivation studies, p.133).

- **Advantages** – it gives a detailed picture of the individual; it can be useful in treating individual problems; it helps in discovering how a person's past may be related to the present; it can form the basis for future research; by studying those who are unusual, psychologists can discover more about what is usual.
- **Disadvantages** – it relies on memory, which may be poor or distorted; the information gained about one person cannot be generalised to apply to other

people; it relies on participants telling the truth; the interviewer may be biased if they are looking for certain information.

Surveys

A survey asks people questions, either through face-to-face **interviews** or written **questionnaires** (see Stress, p.144). The questions must be carefully prepared so that they are clear, and do not persuade the respondents (the people answering the questions) to answer in a particular way. The researcher might first do a pilot study with the questions, giving them to a few people and asking for comments. If the questions are unclear or produce biased answers, the researcher can adjust them for the main study.

In order to reduce **demand characteristics** (see p.180) which might encourage participants to give the answers they think the researcher wants, surveys are often given general titles such as 'A study of children's toys' when the survey is actually trying to find out whether parents encourage their children to play with toys related to their gender. In addition, a few questions may be included which give the impression the survey is about something else, perhaps asking how much the parent spends on toys or the child's attitude to books. Answers to these questions are noted but not counted as data.

The questions may be closed or open-ended, depending on the kind of information the researcher wants:

- **Closed questions** produce clear-cut answers which are easy to interpret and quantify, such as 'Is your child happy at school? – yes/no?'. Respondents may want to answer 'Well, it depends', yet because they are forced to choose yes or no, their answer will not reflect their real opinions. A compromise is the question which provides a range of answers, perhaps using a scale from 1–5 to reflect the strength or amount of agreement. This provides more detailed information which is still easy to quantify (see Figure 11.2, p.149).
- **Open-ended questions** give the respondent the opportunity to provide a lot of information and are useful for in-depth research: for example, 'What do you think of your child's school?'. However, it would be difficult to compare with other people's answers, so the open-ended question is less useful when trying to quantify information.

Questionnaires

Because they require written answers, questionnaires depend on respondents being able to read and understand correctly. They may be distributed by hand, by post or from a distribution point such as a doctor's surgery or supermarket. Once completed they can be returned by post or collected by hand.

Questions can be closed or open-ended (see p.176) but must be clear, unambiguous and understandable. Respondents should remain anonymous, so they must not be asked to give their names.

- **Advantages** – questionnaires are quick and easy to operate; a very large sample can be used; people who are geographically distant can be studied; questionnaires can open up new ideas for further research.
- **Disadvantages** – the sample will be biased because it relies on people returning the questionnaires (they may be returned by people who have plenty of time or strong feelings about the topic); people may not give honest or accurate answers due perhaps to misunderstanding or boredom; people may not understand the questions correctly or indeed return the questionnaires at all.

Interviews

Here the researcher asks the questions face-to-face and the structure of the interview can vary:

- **Structured interviews** consist of a series of fixed questions with a limited range of possible answers, much like a questionnaire. They are the fastest to complete and if well prepared they provide data which is easy to quantify and analyse; but they suffer from the drawbacks of closed questions.
- **Semi-structured interviews** comprise open-ended questions which cover the information the researcher wants to gain. However, respondents may provide this information without being asked a specific question, so the researcher is flexible about the questions themselves, and the order in which they are asked. This style is useful for gaining more in-depth and accurate information from respondents, but it is more difficult to compare answers.
- **Clinical interviews** are the most informal and in-depth technique; they enable the interviewer to re-phrase questions if necessary, to ask follow-up questions or clarify answers that are ambiguous or contradictory. This technique was used by Piaget in his work with children (see pp.77–8) and may be used in the diagnosis of mental disorders. Although this technique provides detailed information, its results should not be generalised to the population as a whole, and it is possible that the interviewer may bias the response or misinterpret the answers that are given.

- **Advantages** – in semi-structured and clinical interviews the interviewer can clarify questions and ambiguous answers; there is a very high rate of return; sampling can reflect the general population's characteristics.

● **Disadvantages** – answers may be biased by the way questions are asked or how they are clarified; respondents may give the answers they think the interviewer wants; they may give answers they think are socially acceptable rather than truthful; this is a slow and expensive method.

Content analysis

In content analysis, researchers analyse the content of a communication such as a conversation, television programme, news report, advertisement or newspaper article. This method has been used in research on topics such as racism, gender stereotyping and aggression.

As an example, to analyse levels of aggression in two children's cartoons, acts of aggression would have to be coded (such as pushing, hitting), the intensity of the act might be rated from 1 (slight push) to 3 (hard push – victim falls down), and the length of time each act lasted might be noted. Results would show the total number of each type of aggression, what percentage of the cartoon time was spent on each act, and so on. So content analysis produces quantitative information, because the information can be expressed as numbers.

● **Advantages** – it enables psychologists to collect data on how the media or other people may influence our attitudes and behaviour; by reducing complex information to simple numbers it is much easier to make comparisons.
● **Disadvantages** – it can be difficult to decide what aspects of the communication are to be coded, and how; the process of content analysis is very time-consuming; by focusing on what can be coded or measured, the meaning or context of the material is omitted, and this may be important.

Experiment

This is where psychologists start meddling! The experiment has been widely used in psychology because the psychologist has greater control over what happens and can therefore test cause and effect. The experimenter alters one variable (called the **independent variable**), and then measures what effect this has on another variable (called the **dependent variable**).

Independent variable (IV) and dependent variable (DV)

We can take the experiment on infant perception conducted by R. Fantz (1961) as an example (see Form or pattern perception, p.131). He presented infants with two visual stimuli side by side, such as a plain black square and a black/white check pattern. The two visual stimuli were the independent variable (the IV), because this is what he was manipulating.

If the infant looked at the pattern longer than the plain black square, Fantz thought this would indicate that the infant could perceive pattern, so he measured how long the infant looked at each stimulus. In other words, to find out whether the IV (the two stimuli he manipulated) had any effect, he measured the time spent looking at each of them. So the time spent looking was the dependent variable (the DV).

The dependent variable *depends* on what the researcher manipulates, and it is what the researcher measures. It enables researchers to decide whether their manipulation did in fact have an effect.

Measuring the dependent variable

When planning their research, psychologists must decide how to measure the dependent variable. These measures might be, for example, the time spent looking, the number of words recalled, the time taken to complete a task, the number of positive reinforcements or the level of shock given.

Measuring behaviour is more complex: for example, measuring aggression. The psychologist needs to define what behaviours are to be considered aggressive. For example: pushing – how hard?; facial expressions – which ones?; verbal behaviour – what kind? How will the behaviour be measured – how often it occurs or how long it lasts, or both?

Controlling other variables

To be confident that the IV has indeed caused the DV, the researcher must control all other aspects of the experiment – must control other **variables**. In Fantz's experiment, if some infants saw the patterns in good light and others dim light, this could affect the time spent looking and so confound the results. This variation in the amount of light is a **confounding variable**, i.e. anything which systematically affects the results. Some of the other variables which researchers need to consider are:

● **Situational variables** – these are aspects of the environment which may affect the participants' behaviour in the experiment, such as the variation in light described above. Other variables could be the time of day, whether others are present, or background noise. Situational variables should be controlled to ensure that they are the same for all participants.

- **Participant variables** – this refers to the ways in which each participant differs from the others, and how this could affect the results. For example, if participants doing a word memory task were tired, dyslexic or had poor eyesight, this could affect their performance and the results. Researchers try to ensure that such variables are evenly distributed between the research groups. The method of doing this is described under Experimental design on p.181.
- **Standardised procedure** – this means that each participant is treated in exactly the same way, each doing exactly the same tasks, with the same materials, in exactly the same order. This reduces the **variables** in the procedure.
- **Standardised instructions** – each participant must be given exactly the same instructions, ideally by the same person and in the same way. If some participants were given instructions which included a demonstration of how to do a task, and others were not, this could affect the results. One way of ensuring standardisation is to provide written instructions, which should be simple and clear.

Types of experiment

We have just looked at how to measure and control variables, but in reality psychologists never have full control of all the variables. This becomes apparent as we examine the different types of experiment described below.

Laboratory experiment

In the laboratory experiment there is a high level of control of **variables**; the work of Fantz is an example. The psychologist manipulates the **IV** (the independent variable), decides where the experiment will take place, at what time and with which participants, in what circumstances, and using a standardised procedure. This standardisation may create **demand characteristics**. These are features of the research which may affect participants' behaviour, so they may act unnaturally or look for cues to tell them what the research is about and behave accordingly (see Milgram's research on p.9).

Field experiment

In a field experiment the psychologist manipulates the **IV** but the experiment takes place in a real-life setting, so there is less control over **variables** such as the people who take part or when the study happens. In the experiment by Felipe and Sommer (1966) confederates invaded the personal space of people sitting in a library (see p.18). The IV was the positions in which the invader sat, but the researchers could use only people who were already sitting alone in a library at a particular time, so control over **participants** and environment was limited.

Quasi or natural experiment

The quasi or natural experiment is one in which the independent variables occur in real life, so the researcher cannot 'create' a difference for the purpose of the experiment. Naturally occurring **IVs** include age, gender, race or place of work. For example, in Cottington's (1983) comparison of stress in workers from noisy and less noisy factories, the noise levels were the IV but these were already established (see p.151). The researchers could not create two factories (with workers) which were identical except for the level of noise; they had to use noise levels in two factories which already existed, and this reduced the amount of control they could exert.

You will see below that what is a disadvantage in one type of experiment becomes an advantage in another.

- **Advantages** – in a laboratory experiment it is possible to test cause and effect; this is less true with quasi experiments and much less true in field or natural experiments, so researchers have to be very cautious in interpreting their results in these latter cases; in the field and natural experiments researchers can see how people behave naturally as a result of the manipulation.
- **Disadvantages** – because laboratory experiments are artificial, this may affect participants' behaviour and produce results which do not apply to real life; as participants know they are taking part in an experiment they may be affected by **demand characteristics**; people, particularly children, do not always follow instructions exactly; in natural and field experiments the researcher cannot be sure that the results are due to the manipulation because there are so many other uncontrolled variables.

Experimental design

In an experiment data is compared from two (or sometimes more) sources. In the Fantz experiment the data was the amount of time the infant spent looking at the black square and at the pattern. But often the source of data is the two groups of participants, as in Cottington's study of stress. Here one group was workers at the noisy factory, the other was workers from the less noisy factory.

Sometimes one group experiences the IV (called the **experimental condition**) and the other group does not (this is the **control condition**). In Bandura's research into the imitation of aggression, children were allocated to either a control condition (participants watching a race) or the experimental condition (participants who watched a film of an adult being aggressive).

The way in which participants are assigned to groups is called the **experimental design**. The three types of experimental design are described below.

Independent measures design

Here there are different participants in each group. In **quasi** or **natural experiments** the groups are naturally occurring, so participants can go into only one of the two groups (as happened in Cottington's stress experiment). In **laboratory** and some **field experiments** the researcher is manipulating the IV and is able to choose which participants are assigned to the experimental group and which to the control group. This should be done by **random allocation**, which ensures that each participant has an equal chance of being assigned to one group or the other (for details of randomising, see Sampling on p.191).

However, people vary in their experiences, attitudes, intelligence, alertness, moods – these are **participant variables**. Because participants are assigned randomly, the researchers do not know whether one group comprises most of the more alert or skilled participants. If this was the case, these participant variables might cause differences between the results from the two groups which are not related to the IV. A large **sample** is needed to reduce this effect.

If there is a variable that may directly affect the results (such as eyesight) then a pre-test should be done to ensure that the variable is equally distributed between the two conditions. For example, after all participants have had an eye test, both groups should comprise the same number of participants with poor eyesight and good eyesight.

- **Advantages** – the independent measures design is the quickest and easiest way of allocating participants to groups; there are no **order effects** (which occur with repeated measures, see below).
- **Disadvantages** – participant variables may affect the results, but using a large sample to counteract this makes the research more expensive and time-consuming, as does a pre-test.

Repeated measures design

Here every participant goes through the **experimental** *and* the **control** conditions. This is an advantage because as the same people are in both conditions there are no participant variables or need for pre-testing. However, there is a drawback: participants may behave differently after they experience one condition and thus affect the results – this is called **order effects** or **practice effects**.

To get around this problem the researcher **counterbalances** the order of the conditions for the participants. The sample is split into two: one half does the experimental condition (A) then the control condition (B); the other half does the control condition (B) then the experimental condition (A). This is called the ABBA design; it cancels out any order effects.

- **Advantages** – repeated measures design eliminates the effect of participant variables; it is therefore possible to have a fairly small sample.
- **Disadvantages** – because of order effects, counterbalancing must be employed; participants may decide not to return for the second part of the experiment; this design cannot be used in quasi or natural experiments because participants automatically fall into one of two conditions.

Matched pairs design

This uses different participants in each group but they are matched in pairs on the basis of variables relevant to the study, such as age, gender, intelligence, reading ability or socioeconomic background. This may require pre-tests in order to ensure good matching. One of each pair is then assigned to the **experimental condition** and the other to the **control condition**. The perfect matched pairs design is one which uses identical twins.

- **Advantages** – a fairly small sample will be enough, though more participants will be needed to go through the pre-tests in order to find good matches; the effects of individual differences are reduced; there are no order effects; it can be used in quasi experiments by matching participants in the important variables *except* for the IV: for example, a male and a female would be matched on the basis of age, intelligence, socioeconomic background.
- **Disadvantages** – it can be expensive and time-consuming; accurate matching is quite difficult, participant variables may still affect results.

Correlational study

Sometimes psychologists want to find out what behaviours go together: for example, to see whether the amount of violent television watched is related to the amount of aggression shown. Both the variables may already be occurring, but in order to find out if they are related the psychologist must measure the variables and then calculate a correlation. The data may have come from questionnaires or observations, for example. There are two patterns of correlation:

- **A positive correlation** occurs when one variable increases as the other *increases*.
- **A negative correlation** occurs when one variable increases as the other *decreases*.

The relationship can be plotted on a scattergram (see p.197 for examples). If there is no upward or downward pattern in the scores, the indication is that the two variables are not related – this is a zero correlation. It is important to remember that a correlational study can only show a relationship between two variables; we cannot assume that one variable *causes* the other.

- **Advantages** – a correlational study provides information about variables which cannot be controlled; it may form the basis for a follow-up study to test cause and effect; the value of one variable can be predicted from the other one; a correlational study can be used when it would be unethical to conduct an experiment: for example, to see whether there is a correlation between an individual's age and the intensity of their phobia.
- **Disadvantages** – it is not possible to find out whether one thing causes another, only whether the two variables are related.

Longitudinal study

A longitudinal study enables researchers to study the same individuals over a period of time, just as Tizard, Rees and Hodges (1978) investigated the development of children in institutionalized care up to eight years of age.

- **Advantages** – a longitudinal study permits the comparison of the long-term effects of an experience; changes which are common to most people can be identified; characteristics which persist and those which tend to disappear can be identified; there are no participant variables; people can be studied in considerable depth.
- **Disadvantages** – some participants will drop out over the years, so their data will be of limited use; long-term funding is necessary and may be hard to find; it is difficult to change the study once it is under way; findings may be out of date by the conclusion of the study; social change at any stage in the study may affect the variables being measured.

Cross-sectional study

A cross-sectional study also investigates change over time, but does so by comparing people who are at different ages or stages and studying them all together. For example, to study changes which occur as children grow up, 4-, 8-, 12- and 16-year-olds can be studied at the same time. In contrast, a longitudinal study would take 12 years to complete.

- **Advantages** – it provides immediate results; it is cheaper than the longitudinal study; there is less likelihood of participants dropping out; there are less likely to be major changes in the lives of participants which would affect results.

● **Disadvantages** – there are individual differences between groups which can bias results (although a large sample will reduce this); social changes may create differences between groups (the seven-year-olds may have experienced major educational change which the 12-year-olds have not); it tends to exaggerate differences between ages.

Conducting research

Other chapters in this book describe research carried out by psychologists. Sometimes weaknesses in the research are identified, but where they are not you will be able to evaluate the research by referring to the material in this chapter. You will find this useful when you take the exam.

As part of your course you also have to plan and carry out your own research. Use the material in this chapter to help you decide which method is the most appropriate for what you want to do, and use the next chapter to help you plan and write up your research.

The OCR exam

The OCR exam will test your knowledge of:

● a range of psychological methods: observation, case study, survey, experiment, correlation, content analysis, longitudinal and cross-sectional studies
● advantages and disadvantages of these methods.

Several of the sample exam questions in earlier chapters include questions which test your knowledge of the topics listed above.

Planning, Carrying Out and Writing Up an Investigation

When psychologists want to find out more about a topic they first read the work of other psychologists. They may find that nobody has studied exactly what interests them, or that someone has but there were flaws in the study which affected the results. They would then plan their own research, recording what they do and what they find, then write it up as a report. This may be published in a psychology journal so that other psychologists can read it and benefit from it, and this is how psychological knowledge is spread and developed. This chapter is written to help you to plan, carry out and write up your own research. It starts with information on ethics, because you should be mindful of ethical concerns as you plan and carry out each stage of your investigation.

Ethics

Ethics are the standards of behaviour that we use in our dealings with others. To behave ethically when conducting research, we must treat others with respect and concern for their wellbeing, we must not take advantage of their trust or their lack of knowledge. Unethical behaviour discredits psychology and the work of other psychologists. People may refuse to help with future research if they have been offended by unethical experiments. Ethical concerns apply to both humans and animals, though our focus here is on humans.

Ethical guidelines have been drawn up by the British Psychological Society (BPS) and the Association for the Teaching of Psychology (ATP). These are summarised below under the four Cs – competence, consent, confidentiality and conduct. Remember these when planning your research and check with your teacher that your plans are within these ethical guidelines.

Competence

You must work within your limits and must be very cautious about giving advice, as people tend to think that anyone studying psychology is able to advise them on their problems.

Consent

Participants should be volunteers and be informed what the research is about and what they will be asked to do before they are asked to consent to take part – this is **informed consent**. People should not be **deceived** into taking part by being told the study is about something else, or by ignoring aspects of the study which might affect their willingness to take part. Information should be withheld only if there is no other way of carrying out the research. This deception should not persuade the participant to give consent which they would later regret. Full details should be given during the participant's debriefing.

Participants should be told they have the **right to withdraw** from a research study at any time, and be reminded of this right during a long study or if the participant appears to be distressed or uncomfortable. The researcher should stop the study if participants are uncomfortable or distressed, even if they have not asked to withdraw.

After the research, participants should be **debriefed** so they know what the study was about; their own results should be available to them and the researcher must answer any questions.

Some people may be unable to give informed consent, such as children or those with special needs. Nevertheless, they must be asked if they are willing to help you, but full consent must be gained from whoever is responsible for that person, such as a parent or carer. These people must be given full information, just as if they were the participants, before being asked for their consent.

Research which is to be carried out in an institution such as a school, factory or supermarket must also be approved by the responsible authority in the institution.

Consent is not necessary when **observing** people in public, as they could be observed by anyone. Nevertheless, such observations could be intrusive or unnerving, so they should be carefully planned to avoid this.

Confidentiality

Information about the identity of the participants and any data gained from them must remain **confidential**. It is unethical to give information about a participant to someone else (such as another researcher) without that person's consent. Data should not be accessible to others and participants should be identified by a number or letter in the research report, in order to protect their **anonymity**.

Conduct

Researchers must ensure that any equipment is safe to use, and that participants are not asked to do anything that is illegal or might cause them physical harm. Nor should participants experience psychological harm, such as distress, fear, anger, embarrassment, offence. Great care should be taken with children, as they are particularly vulnerable and may be unhappy or harmed by experiences that adults would find problem-free.

All participants should leave the investigation feeling as good about themselves as when they started it.

Researchers should be honest about their abilities and competence. They must never make up their own data or use someone else's data and claim it is their own.

The research report

Chapter 13 provides details about various research methods. Use that information to help you plan your own investigation. The remainder of this chapter will help you in the planning and carrying out of your investigation: it does this as it tells you how to write up your investigation.

There are a number of ways of writing a research report, but information is usually provided under the following headings in this order:

- **Title**
- **Introduction** (including **Hypothesis** or **Research Aims**)
- **Method** (including **Design**, **Participants**, **Materials** and **Procedure**)
- **Results**
- **Discussion**
- **Appendix**
- **References** or **Bibliography**.

Information about what to include in each of these sections is given through the rest of this chapter, which ends with a summary of the marks you can gain for writing a good report.

Title

The title page should indicate what your report is about: for example, 'An observational study of gender differences in children's play' or 'An investigation into conservation of liquid'. You should also give your name on this page.

Introduction

The introduction states the aim of the research and provides the background to your investigation, describing the theory and research upon which your own work is based. Ensure that any theories or research included in your Discussion have already been described here in the Introduction.

Finally you state the aim of your study and the hypothesis. For example, if you want to find out whether organisation of words improves recall, you could write:

Research aim The aim of this research is to investigate whether organisation of words improves the number recalled.

Hypotheses

If you want to manipulate a variable, such as age (the **independent variable**), to see if this affects the children's answers (the **dependent variable**), then you will be conducting an **experiment**. Here you are testing an expectation – we say that you are testing a hypothesis. The hypothesis is a statement of what you expect to happen. An experiment on improving memory could investigate whether people recall more words if they see them in an organised arrangement rather than a random list (see p.120). In this case the hypothesis would be:

The experimental hypothesis is that participants who see words organised by meaning will remember more words than participants who see the same words listed in random order.

You should also state the independent variable and the dependent variable underneath. For example, you could write:

The **independent variable** is the way the words are presented.
The **dependent variable** is the number of words recalled.

If you have used a non-experimental design such as a naturalistic observation or a **correlational study** there is no independent variable, but you will still have an expectation which you are testing. This expectation is called the research hypothesis, and two examples are:

The **research hypothesis** is that males are more likely to sit next to other people and females are more likely to sit opposite other people.

The **research hypothesis** is that there will be a correlation between the number of people in a group and the level of conformity shown by an individual.

In this example you would expect that the more people in the group, the higher the level of conformity. This would be a **positive correlation** (see p.183 for more details) and you could insert the word 'positive' before 'correlation' in the research hypothesis.

Method

In this section you describe exactly what you did so that somebody else would be able to replicate your research from your description. Divide the method into four sub-sections as shown below.

Design

Provide details of the framework of the study. Identify and describe the **research method** you used and say why you chose it. See Chapter 13 for details.

For an experiment state the **experimental design** you used (see p.181) and why it was the most appropriate. Briefly describe what each group did; this means describing how the **independent variable** was put into effect. If you **counterbalanced**, say how you did so. Also state how you measured the **dependent variable**, and what controls you used.

With a non-experimental design there is no direct manipulation of an independent variable but you must mention any controls you implemented, such as checks for inter-observer reliability.

Mention the pilot study if you conducted one, briefly describe what you did, what you learned from it and how this affected your final design.

Participants

Here you explain how you selected the participants in your study. These are your **sample**. They should represent the target population, which could be, for example, six-year-olds, male adults, people sitting alone, insecurely-attached children or heart-attack victims. If your sample represents the target population, you can generalise your results to the people in that target population.

Psychologists decide on the size of their sample by taking account of factors such as the experimental design (**independent measures** require more participants than **repeated measures**) and time available (a small sample is usual in an **observational** study because such a study is time-consuming and no hypothesis is being tested). Although a larger sample is more representative of a population, most researchers are limited by time and cost to perhaps 30 or 40 participants, and you will need fewer than this in your research.

Before selecting participants you must decide if there are any characteristics which might affect someone's eligibility: in a study of visual perception your participants should all be sighted; in a study of memory for a list of English words, participants must be able to read English.

Once the numbers and characteristics of the participants have been decided they can be selected using one of the three sampling methods described below. These describe how a psychologist would select their sample but your own sample will be much smaller.

Random sampling

Be warned, this is not what you think it is – random sampling is highly controlled! It means that every member of the target population has an equal chance of being selected. For instance, in a study with a target population of seven-year-olds, the names of seven-year-olds from different types of primary schools (inner city, suburban, private and so on) would be gathered. Let us say there are 75 children.

Each child must have an equal chance of being selected, so the names of all the children might be written on a slip of paper and put in a box. To select 20 participants, the first 20 names taken out of the box would comprise the sample. Alternatively, each child might be given a number and the participants could be selected using a random number table, an extract of which is shown in Figure 14.1. To do this, start at any point in the table and move through it either horizontally or vertically. Stop at each number: the child who has this number becomes a participant. When 20 **participants** have been selected they are the sample. This method can also be used to allocate participants in an **independent-measures** design of experiment.

- **Advantages** – results can be generalised to the target population; a large sample is not necessary.

- **Disadvantages** – this method can be time-consuming; people may not agree to take part once they have been selected; you cannot use random sampling in some types of research, such as field experiments or questionnaires.

03 47 43 73 86	39 96 47 36 61	46 98 63 71 62	33 26 16 80 45	60 11 14 10 95
97 74 24 67 62	42 81 14 57 20	42 53 32 37 32	27 07 36 07 51	24 51 79 89 73
16 76 62 27 66	56 50 26 71 07	32 90 79 78 53	13 55 38 58 59	88 97 54 14 10
12 56 85 99 26	96 96 68 27 31	05 03 72 93 15	57 12 10 14 21	88 26 49 81 76
55 59 56 35 64	38 54 82 46 22	31 62 43 09 90	06 18 44 32 53	23 83 01 30 30
16 22 77 94 39	49 54 43 54 82	17 37 93 23 78	87 35 20 96 43	84 26 34 91 64
84 42 17 53 31	57 24 55 06 88	77 04 74 47 67	21 76 33 50 25	83 92 12 06 76
63 01 63 78 59	16 95 55 67 19	98 10 50 71 75	12 86 73 58 07	44 39 52 38 79
33 21 12 34 29	78 64 56 07 82	52 42 07 44 38	15 51 00 13 42	99 66 02 79 54
57 60 86 32 44	09 47 27 96 54	49 17 46 09 62	90 52 84 77 27	08 02 73 43 28
18 18 07 92 46	44 17 16 58 09	79 83 86 16 62	06 76 50 03 10	55 23 64 05 05
26 62 38 97 75	84 16 07 44 99	83 11 46 32 24	20 14 85 88 45	10 93 72 88 71
23 42 40 64 74	82 97 77 77 81	07 45 32 14 08	32 98 94 07 72	93 85 79 10 75
52 36 28 19 95	50 92 26 11 97	00 56 76 31 38	80 22 02 53 53	86 60 42 04 53
37 85 94 35 12	83 39 50 08 30	42 34 07 96 88	54 42 06 87 98	35 85 29 48 38
70 29 17 12 13	40 33 20 38 26	13 89 51 03 74	17 76 37 13 04	07 74 21 19 30
56 62 18 37 35	96 83 50 87 75	97 12 25 93 47	70 33 24 03 54	97 77 46 44 80
99 49 57 22 77	88 42 95 45 72	16 64 36 16 00	04 43 18 66 79	94 77 24 21 90
16 08 15 04 72	33 27 14 34 90	45 59 34 68 49	12 72 07 34 45	99 27 72 95 14
31 16 93 32 43	50 27 89 87 19	20 15 37 00 49	52 85 66 60 44	38 68 88 11 80

Figure 14.1 An extract from random number tables

Opportunity sampling

Researchers use opportunity sampling because it is quick and cheap in comparison with other methods. Anyone who is available, and agrees to take part in research, can become a participant. Opportunity sampling also occurs in **field experiments** such as Felipe and Sommer's study of personal space (see p.17), because participants were people who happened to be sitting by themselves in a library. However, they are unlikely to be a representative sample and were unable to give their consent.

Selecting names from a telephone directory is another example of opportunity sampling. This is not a representative sample, however, because many people who have phones are not listed in a directory and some other people do not have phones.

- **Advantages** – it is easy and fast; it is used in natural and field experiments.
- **Disadvantages** – the sample is unlikely to be representative; people may be asked to take part simply because they look approachable and co-operative; in order to increase representativeness, a large sample is necessary.

Self-selected sampling

A self-selected sample is one where participants choose to take part: for example, people who return questionnaires or who have volunteered to take part in a study (by responding to advertisements in newspapers or on the radio).

- **Advantages** – people offering to take part are less likely to drop out; surveys enable you to have a large sample; they are easier and cheaper to conduct because you do not have to go through a selection process.
- **Disadvantages** – a self-selected sample is unlikely to be representative of the population as a whole; they are likely to be people who have more time, they may be more outspoken, have strong feelings about the topic you are researching and so on; as the sample may be biased, results will be biased, so they cannot be generalised to the population as a whole.

When planning you must decide which sampling method is best for your investigation. Under 'Participants' you state the number of participants, what sampling method was used and why. Say how participants were assigned to groups and give relevant details of participants where possible, such as age, gender, occupation.

Materials

Describe any materials, equipment or apparatus used, such as a tape recorder, selection of photographs, word list. Explain why they were chosen, how answers to questions were marked, and so on. If diagrams or sketches give useful detail, attach these as an Appendix. Copies of **questionnaires** or **observational schedules** should also be attached as an Appendix, along with the marking or scoring system if relevant.

Procedure

Describe how you carried out each step of the investigation in a clear, detailed and logical way. Someone else should be able to repeat what you did by following this description. You should include the following if they are relevant:

- The instructions you gave to your participants (**standardised instructions**).
- How you **controlled variables** such as the time of the study, whether participants were alone or not, how noisy it was, how long participants were given.
- Any **ethical** points which you had to consider and how you addressed them.

Ethics

Describe the ethical considerations that you had to take into account as you planned and carried out your investigation. Refer to the beginning of this chapter for a summary of ethical guidelines in psychology and make sure that you check all your plans with your teacher before you proceed. In your report, you will need to explain in detail how the ethical guidelines were applied to your investigation. For example:

- Decide what you will tell your participants about the research, before you gain their consent. If there is anything they might be uncomfortable about, then make sure that you make this clear to them before you ask if they consent. Write down what you will say, so that every potential participant has complete and accurate information.
- If you cannot be completely honest, because this would bias their behaviour as participants, then you must ensure that you use as little deception as possible and that knowing how they have been deceived will not distress them when they are debriefed.
- Think about your debrief, which is when participants have finished taking part and you tell them exactly what the research is about. If it is possible that they will be annoyed or distressed when you debrief them, then some aspect of your investigation is unethical. You must make sure you alter your planned investigation so that it is ethical.
- Ideally participants should be drawn from your own school or college. Ask your teacher whether the Head or Principal's permission must be gained. It may also be necessary to gain permission from parents or guardians; again you should check with your teacher.
- Ensure that your participants will not have to do anything which is unsafe, unpleasant, embarrassing, offensive or distressing.
- Write out the debrief which will be given to each participant after the research, to ensure that they are given accurate and complete information about what they have done, are able to see their results and are assured results will be anonymous and confidential, and are invited to ask anything they want to about the research.
- Ensure that data gathered from your research is anonymous and is kept safe.

Mention the code of conduct you used as guidance, such as those drawn up by the British Psychological Society (BPS), the Association for the Teaching of Psychology (ATP) or the OCR Guidelines for GCSE students.

Results

This is the section of your report where you present the data from your study and analyse it. Very basic data (such as scores from each participant on each question of a questionnaire) should be attached as an Appendix, but the summary of this data should appear in a table in the 'Results' section, clearly labelled so that the reader knows what information the table contains.

This data may then be presented pictorially in various forms, depending on the type of data. Some of the most common are described briefly below:

- **Bar charts** show amounts or the number of times something occurs. Each bar represents a separate category (see p.131, Figure 10.5 for an example).
- **Graphs** show data which changes over time. The regular information goes along the bottom axis and the data which varies along the upright axis (see p.4, Figure 1.1 for an example).
- **Histograms** show the frequency or amount of something, on a continuous scale. For example, the scores in Fig.14.5 (p.197) would be grouped according the number of scores between 0–10, 11–20, 21–30 and so on. The resulting histogram is shown in Fig. 14.2 below. Note that some columns are empty but are still included as part of the continuous scale.

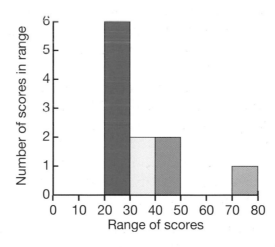

Figure 14.2 Histogram showing number of scores in each range

- **Pie charts** show data as a proportion of the whole. This could be done using Ainsworth's data on children's attachment (see p.61) as shown in Figure 14.3 below.

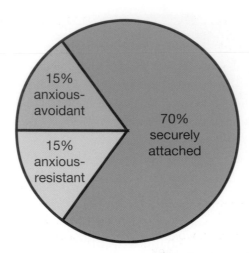

Figure 14.3 A pie chart illustrating the proportions of children showing different types of attachment

- **Scattergrams** show the pattern of relationships in a correlational study. Each axis represents a variable and crosses represent the pairs of scores or ratings. If you draw an imaginary line through the crosses and it goes upwards, this is a **positive correlation**. If this imaginary line runs down, this indicates a **negative correlation**. If there is no upward or downward trend in the crosses, this indicates there is **zero correlation** between the variables – in other words, there is no relationship between them (see Figure 14.4 for examples).

In order to draw conclusions from the data you have gathered, you may need to analyse it. For example, Figure 14.5 shows a set of scores from 11 participants which could be analysed using one or more of the methods described below:

- **The mode** is the number which occurs most frequently in a set of scores; in Figure 14.5 the mode is 26.
- **The median** is the middle number when a set of scores is put in order from lowest to highest; in Figure 14.5 the median is 29.
- **The mean** is what you may know as the average. It is calculated by totalling the scores and dividing that total by the number of scores. For example, the total of the scores in Figure 14.5 is 396, when divided by 11 (the number of scores), the mean is 36. The mean reflects *all* the scores in the data (unlike the **median** and the **mode**). Because of this, it is affected by extreme scores. As an example, if the last score (71) was not counted, the mean of the remaining ten scores would be 32.5.
- **The range** is calculated by taking the lowest score away from the highest score. In Figure 14.5 the range of scores is 48. The range shows the extent to which a set of scores vary.

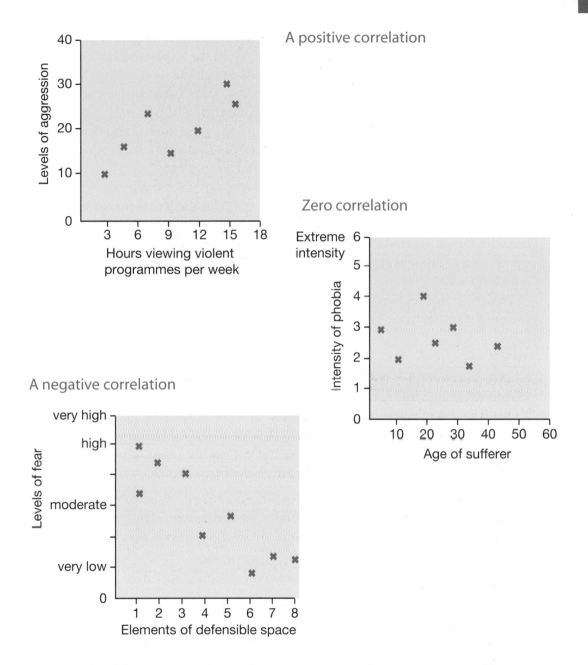

Figure 14.4 Three types of correlations

23, 26, 26, 26, 27, 29, 38, 39, 45, 46, 71

Figure 14.5 A set of scores from 11 participants in an experiment

Calculating the **mean**, **median** or **mode** helps you to draw conclusions from your data. For example, if Figure 14.5 gives scores from the **experimental condition**, but scores from the 11 participants in the **control condition** were all 36, then the mean for both groups would be identical. Despite this, there is clearly an important difference between the two groups. This is best identified by comparing the range of scores for each group, which would be 48 for the experimental and 0 for the control condition. This shows that although data from both conditions produced the same *mean*, scores in the experimental group varied enormously.

We can also find out whether any of the scores are extreme by comparing each score with the mean. For example, in Figure 14.5 all the scores are within 13 of the mean except the highest, which is 34 from the mean. We might decide to analyse the data including this score, then re-analyse it without the highest score. We might get two very different results, perhaps one which supports the hypothesis and one which does not.

Finally in this section, you must state what your main findings are and what they mean in terms of your Aim and Hypothesis.

Discussion

The discussion starts with an explanation of what your results mean and how they relate to the aim or the **hypothesis**. Do they support your hypothesis or not? The results should also be related to the theory and research that was described in your Introduction. Say whether they conform to the theory or challenge it and explain why. Are there any patterns or trends which you can identify? Mention any unexpected findings and consider what could explain them.

Evaluate your own study; ask yourself:

- How did participants respond to your instructions?
- How accurately did your observations reflect what happened?
- Did participants understand the questions in the questionnaire?
- Would a larger sample have made a difference?
- What were the weaknesses in your sampling method?
- Did participants make any useful comments when you debriefed them?
- Were there any confounding variables?
- Were there any ethical issues?

Think about the answers to these questions and what impact they may have had on your results and conclusions. As a result of this analysis, suggest improvements and say how they might affect the results.

Finally, does your study provide any ideas for further research, perhaps because your results challenge your expectations or because you think there may be other reasons for the results?

Appendix

An appendix contains information that is too detailed to put in the main body of the report. A copy of an **observation schedule** or a **questionnaire** with the scoring system would form an appendix. Other appendices could be your **standardised instructions**, an example of a completed questionnaire or detailed results. Each appendix should be identified as A, B, C etc.

References or bibliography

Here you list details of the books, articles and Internet material you read in order to prepare for your research. You give the author, date of publication, title, place of publication and the city in which it was published. Materials from the Internet should include the relevant website address and the date you read it.

The OCR exam

The OCR exam will test your knowledge of:

- ethics
- advantages and disadvantages of a range of psychological methods
- participants and selection
- data collection and interpretation, data presentation – tables, graphs, scattergrams.

Some of the sample exam questions and group activities in earlier chapters include questions which test your knowledge of the topics listed above.

Marks for OCR coursework

Marks will be awarded for the presentation of your report as well as for the content in each section. A description of work which would be awarded the highest marks is given below:

	Maximum marks
Introduction	
The introduction clearly presents relevant psychological concepts, theories and terminology.	5–6
A clear, concise aim and hypothesis are stated and related to the psychology presented in the introduction.	3
Method	
The design is correct and is justified with enough details given to allow the method to be reproduced.	5–6
An awareness of ethical issues has been shown by explaining in detail how ethical issues have been correctly applied to the investigation.	3
Results	
Data is presented logically in appropriate graphs and/or tables. The findings are well summarised and main conclusions clearly evident from the analyses provided. There is a statement which highlights the main findings and which clearly links them to the aims/hypotheses of the investigation.	7–8
Discussion	
Inferences are drawn from the data and these are related both to the aims/hypotheses of the investigation and to the background theory.	4–5
The candidate recognises bias in the information collected and provides an explanation of the way in which this may have affected the results. Suggestions for improvements to the investigation are provided.	3–4
Presentation of report and quality of written communication	
The candidate has used the sections of the report appropriately. There is a good quality of expression throughout with all specialist terms used with a high degree of precision. Very clear written expression.	4–5

Glossary

ageism	discriminating against someone on the basis of their age (p.101)
androgyny	the set of behaviours which includes high levels of both masculine and feminine characteristics (Bem) (p.158)
attachment	a close emotional relationship with another person (p.59)
autonomous morality	morals based on one's own rules and taking account of intent (Piaget) (p.87)
bar chart	a way of illustrating data to show the amounts or number of times something occurs (p.195)
behaviourist	relating to the view that behaviour can be best understood by studying only that which can be observed (p.29)
case study	a detailed study of an individual or a small group (p.175)
cathartic	to rid the body of something negative, such as aggression (p.51)
centration	the tendency to focus on only one aspect of a situation (Piaget) (p.75)
classical conditioning	showing an automatic response to a previously unrelated stimulus (p.33)
clinical interview	a way of finding out about someone's thinking or emotions by using their replies to determine what questions will be asked next, using open-ended, unstructured questions (p.177)
concrete operational stage	the third stage of cognitive development (Piaget) (p.75)
conditioned response	the response that occurs when the conditioned stimulus is presented (p.33)
conditioned stimulus	the stimulus that causes the conditioned response (p.33)
confederate	someone who appears to be a participant but who is actually following the researcher's instructions, so is part of the study (p.5)
conformity	changing one's own ideas or behaviours because of real or imagined group pressure (p.3)
confounding variable	any variable that may systematically distort results (p.179)
conservation	the understanding that something stays the same even though the appearance changes (Piaget) (p.75)

content analysis	a research method which analyses particular features of a communication (p.178)
control condition/ control group	the group of participants who do not experience the IV (p.181)
correlation	a relationship between two variables (p.183)
counterbalancing	giving half the participants the experimental condition first and the other participants the control condition first (p.182)
critical period	the time span during which the individual must be exposed to certain experiences or influences if normal development is to take place (p.62)
cross-cultural research	research which compares people from different cultures (p.134)
cross-sectional study	a study in which different groups are studied at the same time (p.184)
debrief	giving a general explanation of the study to participants when they have finished, answering their questions and ensuring their wellbeing (p.187)
decentre	to be able to take into account more than one aspect of a situation at a time (Piaget) (p.75)
defensible space	territory, centred on the home, which has been designed to protect against intruders (p.25)
demand characteristics	features of the research which may affect the participant's behaviour (p.180)
dependent variable	the outcome of manipulation of the independent variable, the results (p.178)
discrimination	treating people differently simply because they belong to a particular group (p.100)
ego	the part of personality in touch with reality which mediates between the demands of the id and the superego (Freud) (p.40)
ego defence mechanisms	unconscious strategies to reduce anxiety (Freud) (p.40)
egocentrism	seeing the world only from one's own perspective, understanding the world as an extension of oneself (Piaget) (p.74)
Electra conflict	the conflict created by a girl's feelings towards her father (Freud) (p.163)
ethics	desirable standards of behaviour towards others (p.186)
ethnocentrism	viewing other cultures through your own cultural lens and using it as a standard for judging any other culture (p.101)
experiment	a research method in which all variables are controlled except one, so that the effect of that variable can be measured (p.178)
experimental condition/ experimental group	the group of participants who experience the IV (p.181)

extinction	when a conditioned response to a stimulus no longer occurs (pp.34–5)
formal operational stage	the fourth stage of cognitive development (Piaget) (p.77)
frustration–aggression hypothesis	the proposal that frustration always leads to aggression (p.51)
gender	the psychological or cultural aspects of maleness or femaleness (p.157)
gender constancy	the understanding that people stay the same sex despite changes in appearance (Kohlberg) (p.167)
gender identity	the individual's concept of themselves as either male or female (p.157)
gender role	society's expectations about what is appropriate for males and females (p.158)
gender stability	the understanding that one stays the same sex throughout life (Kohlberg) (p.166)
gender typed	in accordance with society's expectations of what is appropriate for males and females (p.158)
generalisation	showing a response to things similar to the conditioned stimulus (classical conditioning) (p.34)
generalise	applying information from one situation to other similar situations (p.175)
graph	a way of representing data to show change over time (p.195)
group norms	the unspoken rules about what is and is not acceptable to members of a group (p.8)
heteronomous morality	moral standards imposed from outside the individual and based on the consequences of actions (Piaget) (p.86)
heterosexism	discriminating against gay men and lesbian women because of their sexual orientation (p.101)
histogram	a way of showing the frequency or amount of something, on a continuous scale (p.195)
hypothesis	a prediction of what will happen, which may be tested in an experiment (p.189)
id	the part of personality that contains our instincts and desires (Freud) (p.40)
identification	the process by which the child comes to take on the ideas and behaviours of the same-sex parent (Freud) (p.163)
imitation	copying behaviour (social learning theory) (p.43)
independent measures	a design of experiment which has different participants in each group (p.181)
independent variable	the variable that the researcher manipulates (p.178)

in-group–out-group	the division of people into two groups: the in-group is the group to which we belong; the out-group is all the others (p.104)
innate	part of our physical make-up at birth (p.130)
learned	a relatively permanent change in behaviour which is due to experience (p.31)
libido	the life instinct (Freud) (p.163)
longitudinal study	a study which follows the same participants over an extended period of time (p.184)
matched pairs	a design of experiment in which each group has different participants but they are paired on the basis of their similarity on several characteristics (p.183)
maternal deprivation	having no attachment, or a damaged attachment, to the mother (Bowlby) (p.65)
mean	average (p.196)
mnemonics	aids to memory (p.121)
model	whomever the individual copies behaviour from (social learning theory) (p.43)
nature	based on innate characteristics (p.130)
negative correlation	a relationship between two variables in which as one increases the other decreases (p.183)
negative reinforcement	anything which strengthens behaviour because it stops an unpleasant experience (p.36)
nurture	our environment, our experiences after birth (p.130)
obedience	following a command, order or instruction which is given by an authority figure (p.9)
object permanence	a child's understanding that although it can no longer see an object, the object still exists (Piaget) (p.74)
observational method	research which involves watching and recording behaviour (p.173)
observational learning	human learning which takes place by observing others, social learning (p.42)
Oedipus conflict	the conflict created by a boy's feelings towards his mother (Freud) (p.163)
operant conditioning	learning which occurs as a result of reinforcement or punishment (p.35)
opportunity sampling	selecting whomever is available to be a participant (p.192)
out-group	those people who do not belong to our own group or in-group (p.104)
participant variables	ways in which individual participants differ from each other and that might affect results (p.179)

perception	the process of interpreting, organising and elaborating on sensory information (p.125)
personal space	the emotionally charged bubble of space which surrounds each individual (p.16)
physlological	related to the processes of the body (p.144)
phobia	an intense, persistent and irrational fear of something which is accompanied by a compelling desire to avoid it (p.31)
pie chart	a way of showing data as proportions of a whole (p.195)
positive correlation	a relationship between two variables in which as one increases the other increases (p.183)
positive reinforcement	anything which strengthens behaviour because it is rewarding (p.37)
practice effect	when participants do better on a task the second time they do it; it occurs in a repeated-measures design of study (p.182)
prejudice	an attitude towards a group, or a member of the group based on characteristics which are assumed to be common to all members of the group (p.97)
pre-operational stage	the second stage of cognitive development (Piaget) (p.74)
proactive interference	memory difficulties which occur when something which is already stored in memory interferes with the ability to take in new information (p.118)
psychoanalytic theory	a theory based on the idea that behaviour is caused by unconscious forces (Freud) (p.39)
punishment	anything that weakens behaviour or makes a behaviour less likely to happen (p.35)
racism	an extreme negative attitude towards someone of another race, combined with feelings of superiority about one's own race (p.101)
random sampling	selecting participants on the basis that all members of the target population have an equal chance of being selected (p.191)
range	the difference between the highest and lowest scores (p.196)
rehearsal	repeating information so that it is retained in memory (p.114)
reinforcement	anything that strengthens behaviour (p.35)
repeated measures	a design of experiment in which the same participants are in the control and the experimental group (p.182)
response	the behaviour that results from a stimulus (p.33)
retroactive interference	memory difficulties that occur when something which is newly-learned interferes with the ability to recall information already stored (p.117)
sampling	the method by which participants are selected for research (p.191)
scattergram	a way of showing the degree to which data is related (p.196)

self-selected sample	a sample comprising participants who choose to take part in research (p.193)
sensorimotor stage	the first stage of cognitive development (Piaget) (p.73)
separation distress	the unhappy response shown by a child when an attached figure leaves (p.60)
sex identity	the biological status of being male or female (p.157)
sexism	discriminating against someone on the basis of their sex (p.101)
social categorisation	classifying people as members of either the in-group or the out-group (p.103)
social identity theory	the sense of who we are which is gained from membership of a group (p.103)
social learning	human learning which takes place by observing others; observational learning (p.42)
standardised instructions	the identical instructions given to each participant in a study (p.180)
stereotype	a shared belief about the characteristics of those who belong to a particular social or physical category (p.98)
stereotyping	categorising someone as a member of a particular group and assuming they have the characteristics which all members of that group are thought to have (p.98)
stimulus	anything (such as an event, object or person) which triggers a change in someone's behaviour (p.33)
stranger fear	an unhappy response shown by a child when a stranger approaches (p.60)
stress	a pattern of negative physiological states and psychological responses occurring in situations where people perceive threats to their wellbeing which they may be unable to meet (p.143)
superego	the part of personality related to morals, to what we know is wrong and to the kind of person we want to be (Freud) (p.40)
survey	a way of gathering information by asking many people the same questions (p.176)
territoriality	behaviour associated with the ownership or occupation of a space or area (p.22)
territory	a physical area which is generally immovable and is owned or controlled by a person or group (p.22)
unconditioned response	behaviour which occurs as the result of a stimulus and over which one has no control, e.g. the fear response (p.33)
unconditioned stimulus	anything which causes an unconditioned response (p.33)
variable	anything which varies (p.178)
vicarious punishment	learning from the way others are punished (p.90)
vicarious reinforcement	learning from the way others are reinforced (p.90)

Further reading

Baron, R., Byrne, D. & Branscombe, N. (2006) *Social Psychology* (11th ed.), Boston, Mass: Allyn & Bacon

Bee, H. & Boyd, D. (2004) *The Developing Child* (10th ed.), Boston, Mass: Allyn & Bacon

Bell, P., Greene, T., Fisher, J. & Baum, A. (2001) *Environmental Psychology* (5th ed.), Fort Worth, TX: Harcourt College Publishers

Cardwell, M., Clark, L. & Meldrum, C. (2003) *Psychology for AS level* (2nd ed.), London: Collins Educational

Coolican, H. (1996) *Introduction to Research Methods and Statistics in Psychology* (2nd ed.), London: Hodder Arnold

Deaux, K., Dane, F. & Wrightsman, L. (1993) *Social Psychology in the 90s* (6th ed.), Pacific Grove, CA: Brooks/Cole

Garfinkel, H. (1967) *Studies in Ethnomethodology*, Eaglewood Cliffs, NJ: Prentice Hall

Golombok, S. & Fivush, R. (1994) *Gender Development*, Cambridge: Cambridge University Press

Gross, R. (2003) *Key Studies in Psychology* (4th ed.), London: Hodder Arnold

Gross, R. (2005) *Psychology: The Science of Mind and Behaviour* (5th ed.), London: Hodder Arnold

Gross, R., McIlveen, R., Coolican, H., Clamp, A. & Russell, J. (2000) *Psychology: A New Introduction for A Level* (2nd ed.), London: Hodder Arnold

Hayes, N. (2000) *Foundations of Psychology* (3rd ed.), Walton-on Thames, Middx: Thompson Learning

Hill, G. (1998) *Advanced Psychology Through Diagrams*, Oxford: Oxford University Press

Malim, T. & Birch, A. (1998) *Introductory Psychology*, London: Macmillan Press

Rutter, M. (1981) *Maternal Deprivation Reassessed* (2nd ed.), Harmondsworth, Middx: Penguin

Smith, P., Bond, M. & Kagitcibasi, C. (2006) *Understanding Social Psychology Across Cultures* (3rd ed.), Hemel Hempstead: Sage Publications

Index